WE MAKE CLOCKS, NOT TIME

Praise for *We Make Clocks, Not Time*

"Gerrard provides a brilliant account and assessment of delusionary thinking and experience from the other side, its inside out. Clear clinical prose transforms insight into an antidote to balance extremes of psychosis ranging from flying high on possibility to being grounded in shame. *We Make Clocks, Not Time* is a survival narrative and mesmerizing story built with language that act and refuses to be acted upon, that 'breaches the haze of suffering that denies us creativity and literature' (Belcourt). "

— **Chris Frey**

"*We Make Clocks, Not Time* tackles the big questions surrounding psychosis from an insider's point of view. Gerrard explores the illness and its wider repercussions on his own terms, and does not limit himself to society's prescribed definitions of sanity and insanity. This book is a must-read, not only for those currently finding their way with psychosis, but also for anyone wanting to expand their understanding of the creative mind."

— **Stephanie Voaden**, *Peer*

"*We Make Clocks, Not Time* is an intimate and contemporary analysis of psychosis, art, mind, and meaning, by a truly exceptional and insightful artist."

— **Matthew Swann**, *Peer, BA (Philosophy of Religion)*

"*We Make Clocks, Not Time* is the voice and story behind a stigmatized label. Through his lived experience, John explores the way we perceive and treat mental health, and challenges your own perception and thoughts of what it means to be human."

— **Steph Clark**, *Art Therapist*

"John F. Gerrard offers a bold, deeply personal, and thoughtful account that explores life experiences which shape, define, and sustain identity and perception. His reflective and contemplative words invite insightful and philosophical conversations towards understanding the complexities of all aspects of health, while emphasizing the importance of compassion."

— **Dena Leigh**, *Primary Educator*

"*We Make Clocks, Not Time* is an expression of the written word beyond wellness and healing. It takes readers on a journey of understanding by refining how mental illness and one's personal perception of social experience can mould self-identity and purpose. John Gerrard's insightful reflections on the importance of intentional language and destigmatization lead readers to connection, understanding, and acceptance. This memoir will impact each reader uniquely as it relates to their own practices, experiences, and gratitude."

— **Brittany Bruce**, *MSW, RSW*

"*We Make Clocks, Not Time* shares insightful perspectives on life, art, and mental illness. Gerrard brilliantly confronts the status quo on mental illness through meaningful short narratives on a unique lived experience with psychosis and masterfully explores the broader human experience. This book is for anyone curious about cultivating a deeper understanding of themselves or their fellow humans."

— **Brooke Russell**, *MSc, PhD Candidate (Clinical Psychology)*

"A beautiful insight into experience and personality—the sort of book that helps us understand minds other than our own in a way that promotes empathy and community."

— **Dr. David Moore**, *BSc(Adv.), MBBS(Hons), FRACGP*

WE MAKE CLOCKS, NOT TIME

My Lived Experience with Psychosis, Creativity, and the Ideas That Have Helped Me

John F. Gerrard

Cover design by Bamff Design with images by John F. Gerrard

ISBN: 978-1-7780501-0-7 (paperback)
ISBN: 978-1-7780501-1-4 (ebook)

First published 2022

"The Artist and Choice" was previously published as a part of a *QOQQOON* webzine.

John F. Gerrard Publishing
Calgary, Canada

johnfgerrard.com

for Jen(n)

"In each of us there is another whom we do not know."

— Carl G. Jung

CONTENTS

A Lens (Preface)

As a visual artist and human I'm interested in engaging in the dialogue about identity and mental health. Although these themes have been relatively constant in my art practice, the ways I've expressed them have changed as I've grown. The COVID-19 pandemic served as a catalyst for me to further shift the direction of my work, which until that point had included writing songs, graphic design, and all sorts of painted and drawn two-dimensional images. I had dabbled with using writing in my drawings previously, but in March 2020 I began a body of text-based visual work that was focused on exploring the issues and concepts that interest me, in a way that would promote further understanding and growth as an artist and as a person.

Since then I've gone through around 800 pieces of paper where I've speculated and elaborated on topics such as free will, identity, and mental health.

I didn't know it at the time, but the work would serve as preparation for the more linear/traditional writing of this book. I sat down one morning with the intention of describing some of my experiences with mental illness, as well as organizing the philosophies I'd been exploring in the text pieces, and then spent the next 10 days or so writing the bulk of this book.

It was wonderful to be so engulfed in the process of transforming thoughts into written words and sentences. An exciting exercise in understanding myself better through the power of making my inner workings tangible. I eventually reached a point where I felt that the writing was finished and so I invited people to give me feedback on the first draft. Perhaps in arrogance, I thought the writing was basically ready for print, after some grammar and flow changes.

However, after looking at the document a week later I realized there was still work to be done. Perception is such a strange thing! Since then I have added sections and clarified parts in hopes to bring more value to the project without losing too much of the initial energy I captured with the first draft.

It's important to me that the work is read as a speculative perspective on these issues and is given the space to spark conversation and not dictate conclusions. There is still so much we have to learn about how our minds operate. My goal isn't to construct or relay an all-encompassing framework for psychosis/madness, or anything else for that matter. What follows is a mix of the ideas that have helped me, and their relationship to my own lived experience.

My hope is that this writing helps you in some way navigate those deep waters of our unknown.

Acknowledgements

Thank you to the different branches of family and friends for all the support over the years. I'm grateful to be sharing this life with you. I am indebted to the Greco family for their insight and support while making this book. Thank you to all the people who helped me by reading early versions of this project and providing feedback. Thank you to all the doctors and nurses who have cared for me, in particular Dr. Selmer. Thank you to the Canadian Mental Health Association for the peer support training which was such a huge help in my recovery, in particular the mentorship I received from Debbie Wiebe. I am undoubtedly missing people. Thank you.

"Let's not try to figure out everything at once."

— Matt Berninger

Whimsical Inner Dialogue

Once I have intuitions, I review what's been presented and decide which of these relationships and connections I think are relevant. Once I agree that an intuition is worthwhile, I decide what I'd like to do with this newly static (though still reviewable) information and proceed accordingly.

I have learned to be careful with trusting conclusions or suggestions automatically. Being in recovery has helped me be skeptical and realistic about how my mind can be wrong. It's important to be open with my conclusions and to avoid unwarranted sureness in inherently grey areas.

This interaction between me and me makes me feel like there is a conversation in all of us. There is an automatic part that creates options and possibilities that the conscious self discovers. We decide what to do with what's been found, maybe inventing essences from what we observe? There's discovery too as we look inward and outwardly. As we think about our thinking we transform what we find. Is there multiplicity to self? Or ... "A part of me apart from me," as Justin Vernon says (1).

My interior life is made external by the creative bridge. Making art is a way for me to explore and integrate what I've called the inner other. By forming objects in the external, I give a concrete voice to the conceptual and the emotional. This tangibility allows me to see myself "through something else," to see what's been hidden or kept, to see what I want to keep and to see what I want to change.

Sometimes when I make art I have a plan that I will follow through with, and sometimes I have a process I wish to enact to generate results (algorithmically?). A lot more frequently though, I don't know where I'll end up or how I'll get there. I trust that my senses and intuition will give me options to make decisions with (2), and that I'll know the appropriate time to freeze this process. It's a process where each mark is a reaction to the one before it. Sometimes it feels like I'm tracing a spirit, like how the spectrum of time is given its designations.

When I make art, is there an origin to what I arrived at? Or do I make new progressions, an original? Do I create something that in all senses and possible worlds doesn't exist yet? Or are the pieces I put together always a puzzle, whose form, whose plan, I just discover?

There is an integration that occurs between a me that has one foot in some mystical place, and a me who is deciding my beliefs. The left hand is dealing the cards, while the right decides how to play what's been dealt. It's a strange pseudo-separation, and even stranger to wonder where the deck came from and what the essence of the game we're playing is.

This integration of givens and novel variables… Is there compromise between these constructs of newness and the playing out of some preordained destiny? I remember now.

I make the symbol, and yes that could be new. The clock we may have invented, but the essences they point to ...

These numbers used for time, these distinguishing notions on a circle—are they empty quantities or archetypal, with character? Do they point to real phenomena like words do to earth, wind, fire, and water? There is a previously determined me, which was given, which I discover and belong to. What of the alchemy between sensory and the conceptual? What can't be represented but only alluded to, and so is impossible to define? Yes, that. That spirit. That essence which is ...

That essence that some think to be some person-made amalgamation. Some fiction, some illusion. What's in a name? The word *soul* has so much baggage. How would I have made my own soul?! What of parts and the whole? Are there no universals, only particulars, no ultimate, only different types of immediate realities? Outside of Plato's cave (the matrix), is there another cave, and another, and so on, or is there a highest light, an ultimate essence for essences? A ceiling for the skies that defies our need for effects to have causes. How strange everything is, how wonderfully strange.

I wonder if we are somehow illusives that emerged from the slow progression of inanimate rather than animate matter? Or does everything have some element of spirit or mind (3)? Animating elements here from the start. Real but beyond endings and beginnings. What are they?

Time may be an illusion, but an illusion exists: it's just not as it seems.

We are stardust and constellations. We are the universe looking at itself. We are this separation that still belongs. We're both many and one, some thirdness, some in-betweenness that cannot be captured by one language, one image, or one lens alone.

And so we talk to each other, and look at each other's art. We animate the material with laughter and conversation. Each with our own goodness to offer, we relay our perspectives. Weary from standing, we fashion our own chairs. Soon "us" and "other" become mindful of the shared ground beneath, recognize that we all face the daunting opponents of suffering and death. Those existential facts which for everyone are as inevitable as the forward unravelling of time.

We make room for each other and learn to communicate for the sake of a bigger picture, to get a better sense of what we're up against. We wield the combining quality of collage and form a sort of mystical window, a channel for the fire-like dynamics of our collective and collaborative life.

With each person's uniqueness undiminished, the singular static oneness shifts into and away from a motion of manyness and multitude. We have arrived just at the right time to capture our becoming, to sense the whole thing start spinning like a marvelous clock, with flickering lenses instead of numbers, each centred around the source of some worthwhile muse.

I'm not always this optimistic. For example, we may share the same ground, but how can I be cut from the same cloth as someone who thinks the ground, the earth, is flat? To value this idea years ago may have been reasonable, but in this day and age? Who *are* these people?

The interpretation of our vision is diverse, and this can be wonderful, but some choices that follow make life worse for others. What of the reason that some of us seem to cause more pain, and some of us cause less? This is significant.

Here we are with choice mechanisms that don't seem to be mechanical at all. Some intervention that pulls people in and out of circumstance. Are there any strings that aren't pulled? Maybe I'd be wise to remember that the so-called cold and irredeemable have a devil on their back called the absence of love.

Damn it all. It may be an equivocation, though it feels like a statement of meaning to say that everything is meaningless. Greater minds than mine have tried to figure all this out.

I have learned something through this writing though, and that is that if I had this all figured out I might be some pseudo-Lord. If there was some inherent framework wouldn't it be exploited? What do I ultimately want? To be saved from what I want. At some point you've got to submit that you're not the third-person perspective personified; you're an animal with projection and alliteration skills.

And although I want the pride from doing it all on my own, I've got to admit that I need help, to be taken care of in some ways. Sometimes it feels like I want to be alone or gone forever, so I don't have the potential to get hurt, or to hurt others again, but I've learned that life is more painful alone, for me and for those I love. A lot of the time I don't realize the ultimate implications of my choices, and I probably wouldn't make them the same way if I did.

But I do what I can with what I've got, and try to be wise and realize that I didn't have today's knowledge when I was making yesterday's decisions. How can I prepare for new realities though, to help change what I give and what I get in positive ways? I wish for mystic connection.

For me that's where creativity comes in, as this wonderful bridge between our immediate and potential circumstances. We can project and map out where we want to go. Figure out what we want to avoid with the safety of a static page. Also, revisit to reframe a past we might have misinterpreted. If we stay open we may not reach our goal but find another one that's great too.

Maybe the higher power out there gave us choice, and we are making decisions that happen to be also tracing their plan. Those villains to be refined and heroes humbled as we dance our way through a narrative trajectory towards balance and goodness. I hope so.

It's o.k. that I've had thoughts I didn't want, which led to the "wrong" beliefs, which motivated the "wrong" actions. It's o.k. that we live in a world where all three of these "things" interact and lead to and from each other (4).

It's o.k. I haven't found the holy grail of views, or the perfect ceramic mug. Maybe it's not about finding more ways to control, but about finding that balance between accepting responsibility and submitting, being passive to blamelessness, to innocence.

I'm going to let myself oscillate that good spirit, that breath which connects conceptual to sensory. Where I can breathe in potentials and breathe out new images, new signs. One at a time. One at a time.

Intuitive Diagram by John F. Gerrard
2021, 48" x 60", Ink on Canvas

A Beginning

As far as I can tell, I was 12 years old when I had my first delusion. At the time I was sure that I had the right explanation for a horrible and persistent pain in my stomach. My explanation was outlandish though. In reality there was a more reasonable perspective that I was unaware of, as this initial madness happened when my mind and body were under a significant amount of stress from what we would later discover to be a dangerous case of appendicitis.

Although it happened over 20 years ago, I can still remember the feel of that day vividly. How every variable in the room seemed to be part of an important puzzle that I was meant to solve. It felt like my body had been invaded by some foreign factor, some enemy I was vulnerable to. I remember lying anxiously in bed, convinced there was a relationship between aliens and the immense and unprecedented disturbance in my physical self. This supposedly looming threat served to explain the all-too-real agony in my body.

The certainty was brief, as I eventually fell back into a state of uncomfortable unknowing. At the time I didn't think to mention this to my parents, because it wasn't something that persisted, and also wasn't something that was easily mentioned. I would soon be admitted to the hospital to have my appendix removed and had moments there that were equally surreal. Luckily though, my mind recovered as my body did. It would be quite a few years before I'd have another significant episode, and a while for me to realize that the falsehood I was certain of when I was 12 was best framed as delusional.

The uneasy truth is that everyone may have the potential to experience a psychotic event. For me, that physical sickness was enough to activate an unwell headspace; for others it might take years of isolation, the death or birth of a child, the trauma of war, etc. We're all unique: everyone is dealt a different set of cards and a different set of propensities. Although my beliefs surrounding the nature of our will are ever developing, there seems to be some amount of choice in how we decide to play those cards we're given. Cards that are continually dealt, whose identities we may or may not have influence in determining.

I smoked cannabis in my early teens, which likely contributed further to my vulnerability (5). However, as much as I lean towards this conviction, we should ask: does drug use initiate mental illness or are mentally ill people drawn to use drugs in order to (self-)medicate? The narrative of the relationship between cannabis and mental illness is complicated, and there are a lot of misconceptions. The language we use to describe it is important. The cannabis didn't *cause* my psychosis, though it's likely that it helped activate it. Just like the appendicitis activated a delusion when I was younger, cannabis was one factor among many that brought into reality a dormant propensity. It's important to note that not everyone who uses cannabis will get sick, that it can be a healthy option for some people. Although if I had known that psychosis was a possible outcome from my use of it, I might have chosen differently. It can be difficult in life to predict the ultimate implications of our immediate decisions.

Now I know that I'm someone with a predisposition to mental illness, and so there's no reason to feel guilt or shame for this. This predisposition was set in stone before I was conscious. It wasn't chosen, and I don't think it makes sense to feel guilty or shameful about things that are beyond our control and awareness, although I wonder what sort of scope we *should* have with our awareness.

These issues of responsibility and free will remain important to me. I find it all endlessly interesting. As much as I learn and grow, I don't think I'll ever know definitively whether I did drugs and became mentally ill, or if I was already ill and therefore drawn to use drugs to cope with one illness that led to another.

Part of my journey has involved learning to be comfortable with unknowns. I've learned that so much of recovery is developing a healthy relationship with the past, and this includes reconfiguring my roles with more realism, moving away from a narrative of shame, of being fundamentally flawed. It's been important to embrace an attitude of self-compassion, by working towards recognizing the reality that mistakes were made because I was learning, and that I did the best I could with the information I had at the time.

Without sounding too much like I'm trying to convince myself of my own innocence, I was self-medicating in my early days with cannabis because there was a problem I was trying to solve. The early years were filled with joy, but also with moments when it felt like everyone else had the script to a movie I had been thrown into. I imagine I'm not alone in this feeling, as a lot of us are tuned into things differently, or with the volume up higher than others. Thankfully, I would eventually find solace through music and the niche-connecting phenomenon known as the internet.

Ultimately, my sensitivity has proven to be like a double-edged sword. Without it I likely wouldn't have my creativity, my empathy, my ability to feel the gigantic good in this world. With it I can be too affected by other people's energies, and fall short of what some people think a man should be. I wonder if genetics works like that? The same brain functions responsible for negative things like madness having positive aspects or potential too?

So much of mental health care seems to entail connecting the right action to the right outcome so you know what changes to make. What is causing a particular effect? Is what I'm feeling a symptom of my illness or a side-effect from my medication? Am I creative because of or despite my illness? In addition, I wonder how much of my identity is chosen, and how much is imposed on me? How much of our identity and truths do we create, and how much do we discover?

Regardless of where I land with these questions and others, my goal is to enable you to understand these issues as I process and reflect on them. One key fact is that I identify as having been psychotic, but it's important to remember that this is not the only fact that defines me as a person. I am many things, things on both sides and in-between things, and like most people I have made my own blend of good and bad decisions.

Not everything is within my control. I can't control my initial thoughts or my handed-down circumstance, my genetics, or the way a clock works so well with time—though I can choose how I use my character traits, be they an imposition or a gift. I can refigure my interpretations of the past to find more practical perspectives, and as for truth and who I am, I can stay open and curious so as to leave room for the possibility of continuing to develop as a person.

Psycho

I often forget how familiar I am with the word *psychosis* now, and that for many people terms like *psychosis, psycho,* and *psychopathy* all fall under the same label. Traditionally, when people use the *psychopath* label they're referring to people who have issues with emotional empathy, whereas that's not part of the definition of *psychosis* (6). I define the delusional aspect of psychosis as a disconnect from reality and with a sureness attached. There are different aspects to psychosis. However, I will be focusing on the delusional aspect as it's the area I have the most experience with.

Regardless of whether a person with a certain diagnosis is or isn't toxic, the stigma attached to mental health issues makes everything more dangerous for the person and the people around them. When there's stigma, people are more likely to be in denial. If people are in denial, they're less likely to get help. When sick people don't get help they stay sick. The more sickness there is, the more of that small percentage there is of the sick who are toxic and may become violent.

When I'm Psychotic

When I'm psychotic, the whole world becomes this intricate puzzle I urgently need to figure out. Each move, sometimes simple muscle movements, has some sort of relevance I can't quite identify. I become sure that there is significance, but not always sure about what the sign is pointing to. Each answer I think I find proves to be incomplete or a misdirection. It's a chase that has no end, because the rules of the chase are being defined by some strange part of me as I run along. There are a lot of letdowns. It's like you're certain there's a huge surprise party waiting for you at the dentist, but when you arrive it's just an ordinary appointment.

In these moments, there is a part of me that wants to be involved in something larger than my life as I've known it. I can find out I was wrong about something, only to make it a stepping stone to some greater truth that seems to be very important to find.

It's natural to want to be involved in something bigger than yourself, but when you wrongfully elevate or degrade your involvement, and maintain a belief even when you're shown evidence that contradicts it, you're in delusional territory.

It's important that I don't mention it out loud, or to anyone but myself, but I'm certain there's going to be a big reveal soon. A party where I'll be applauded for all my efforts to solve the deepest problems of the universe. We've been working together, we in this secret society that communicates with subtle hand and intuitive eye movements.

What Is a Delusion?

A delusion is occurring when your underlying brain processes say, "What about this?" and you believe yourself even though the brain's assessment isn't factual. You feel very sure, even though you don't have evidence to support your position (7).

A delusion may be a belief that isn't shared by the community to which the person experiencing it belongs, though there are beliefs that have yet to be proven by more ultimate views, and also beliefs that are shared but run contrary to available evidence. An important factor in determining what is and isn't delusional is how rigidly the person believes it in the face of conflicting evidence, as well as how appropriate a sureness is, given the realm the belief is dealing in.

A clinical delusion is often very personal, an isolated perspective that doesn't accord with common sense. Different faith groups may disagree with each other, but there is consensus within each group.

The hypothesis that healthy beliefs are those that are shared by others is complicated by the fact that some beliefs may seem outlandish at first, but are eventually proven viable by a more ultimate view. This can make distinguishing truth and untruth in some areas difficult, as our ability to conclude definitively is always elusive. That's why a more reliable way to distinguish between delusion and healthy belief is in what happens to the belief when evidence is given that contradicts it. In areas where there is no evidence one way or another it's inappropriate to claim faith as being knowledge.

Another thing to consider is that some beliefs are unusual but not pathological because they don't impede a person's ability to live their life, which we can use as an indicator of pathology or mental illness. How each of us wants to live certainly varies, and when someone is sick they may want to live in a way that they wouldn't even consider if they were well. The opposite is also instructive. Someone may live a perfectly "normal" life but have inflexible beliefs that have no basis in evidence. So although the person may be happy to live the way they do, their unfounded beliefs may in fact make them delusional.

Inflexible certainty is inappropriate in many areas of life, as we are limited as humans by our individual biases and scopes of knowledge. It's wise to keep this in mind. Each of us lives with a different vantage point, chained to our immediate reality, our own framework for life. Our brains always simulate things to a certain extent which makes it hard to see the world fully and without filters. When we frame our surroundings, there is always some degree of ignorance which mars the frame.

Our lenses reveal and distort our environment, with some of our speculating overlapping with others and some not. There are different groups, each with their own consensus, and some of us are more unbending in our beliefs than others. It's healthy to be certain of a conclusion as long as you recognize that the certainty is based only on what you've learned so far. When someone is in the depths of a delusion, they will cling to the conclusion no matter what contradictory evidence is offered. When I'm delusional, I make rigid judgments which are inappropriate. For example, I may be "sure" that a sports team will win a game. I may be right, I may be wrong, although either outcome is possible.

This question of knowing where our ambiguity is appropriate or not cuts to the heart of what it means to be human, to the nature of truth and how we know it. So when we ask, "What is delusional?" we're led to the broader issues of truth and belief. Who decides what's true? Are there many particular instances of truth, each only relevant based on the context in which it applies, with stable variables based solely on the fact that we say they are so? Or is there a universal truth, *The Truth*, which is confirmed by all or any positions or contexts? Perhaps there are areas of life where this is in fact the case, and other areas where it is not. Attempts to answer these questions have filled books upon books throughout history, and so any definitive answer from me would likely be ironic considering my previous words, and certainly goes beyond the scope of my writing.

Let's think about that last sentence. It's certainly true that this goes beyond the scope of my writing, because I decide what the scope of my writing is. Just like I don't *believe* I am John Gerrard, I *know* I'm John Gerrard. I know because I decide to keep that identity which was given to me by my parents. In both cases, I am the one who decides. To put it another way, I win the game because I define the rules. Yes, you could say that I'm not aware of all aspects of myself, and so maybe my certainty is unfounded. However, I think that one of the facts (and vulnerabilities) of being human is that we are often unaware and unable to determine who we are in all regards. We delegate some of our defining power to the groups we belong to.

Although it may be tempting to mitigate the discomfort of not knowing by reducing matters into neat and complete packages that we can manoeuvre and control, the truth is that we don't have the tools to be definitive, to be sure in certain areas of life. We can have faith, and that faith isn't necessarily problematic—except when it claims to be based on evidence, but then it's not really faith, is it?

When I have faith in something I accept that there's an alternative; I see that there are options, other viable paths, but I choose one over the other(s). When I'm delusional I have a hard time humouring the thought that there are alternatives to my fixed belief.

In science, certain theories can be very likely, though they're still open to changes if subsequent evidence suggests alternative explanations (8). The most stable of claims can be empirically measured and verified: these are things we have a sizable consensus on and agreed-upon units to communicate their validity. We don't always have the same measures of certainty in language to communicate the whole range of our experiences, and so some types of reality are not so easily communicated, shared, and verified with others.

Empirically valid and stable claims require testing and retesting under the same conditions. There is evidence to work with. Based on prior observations we know that if you go too long without water you will die. This is true. If someone disagrees with an objective reality and is shown reputable evidence against their belief, then that's delusional—though it will often be the interpretation and relevance of the data and information that people argue about in order to promote the delusion. There's what is, what we think it implies, and what we think ought to be done with it.

In life we often need to make decisions and take actions based on probabilities and not certainties. It is likely that smoking will cause me harm so I should act accordingly. When I'm experiencing delusions my capacity and ability to critically engage with these decisions are minimized or compromised. The misinformation being experienced not only *feels* real, it *is* my reality. When I'm delusional I'm immersed and unable to step back and reflect rationally. To think about my thinking.

Critical thinking is an important skill for everyone to learn, but is especially crucial for those of us who deal with psychosis. Stepping back from our thoughts helps us analyze their relevance and accuracy. What pops into your head, be it a thought or an emotion, isn't necessarily a truth. Critical thinking takes practice, and requires insight. When forming beliefs, we should ask how they connect to other people's realities, and what someone else would say about these conclusions.

I don't always want to pursue the evidence when I'm delusional. A part of me may realize that I'm wrong, but not want to be proven so. Sometimes I purposefully stay ignorant to maintain a certain safety, or to maintain the pleasantly intoxicating nature of what I'm experiencing.

These delusional beliefs are subjective and based on the story I tell myself about myself, and so they can be hard to prove right or wrong. When I'm sick, my mind has a tendency to shift the story to something else if a delusion is put in doubt. I don't try to prove them wrong per se, or accept the fact that there may be other options that are either just as likely or more likely to be the truth of the matter. This openness is the opposite of being delusional.

I've experienced these mismade narratives in two categories. I either believed I was elevated, a hero of some sort, or I believed I was a villain and that people thought more negatively about me than they actually did. Either way I am far from the position I actually occupy in the world.

When I'm delusional, I sometimes believe myself to be a hero for five minutes, and then for the next five I'm the villain. Sometimes I'm the hero or villain for much longer. Why? I'm not sure. Maybe I'm experiencing a part of the self a lot of people don't have access to. Maybe my inner other is trying to tell me something important. Maybe it's just an uncomfortable or comforting noise.

Theory aside, I know how painful it can be to experience a psychosis. Both in the experience of it, and in how you're treated afterwards, by others and by yourself. It's not uncommon for someone to fall into a depression after a psychotic episode. The examples we hear about people who have psychoses are usually so negative. You hate that you're a part of that group. The shame disconnects you.

I may be biased, but I think it's important we show compassion to people who suffer from delusions, or who are tuned into life differently. It can be both terrifying and intoxicating, but more importantly to mention again and again is that it is isolating. We should help our unwell find stable ground again and work towards consensus without invalidating their lived experience. Being someone who has experienced psychosis, I need to remind myself that I deserve to have these attitudes towards myself. It's hard to avoid feeling shameful, when a big portion of society has labelled you as fundamentally "other."

Having had psychosis and wanting those struggles to have purpose, I wonder if there's been anything meaningful in my madness. At this point, I would say it depends if you think of it as noise or not, and this I think would depend on how you view "normal" thinking as well. The purpose of our thinking is hard to pin down. We can say that we think to survive, for power (9). That we think to learn, to evolve. Whatever we suggest as an explanation leads to another question: why that?

Where do all the options of what there is to conceptualize come from? Are there archetypes that make up a sort of card deck (10)? Or are the perceptions truly new, unique, and we're artists with pen in hand, writing and inventing the concept of heroes and villains? All to echo our own need to have things to embrace and things to expel.

Meaning may be made or it may be discovered by us. Either way, it doesn't have to be "handed down" to be, well, meaningful. I can make connections from the noise, connect variables that aren't relevant universally, but that are meaningful to my particular situation. Though personally I don't want to create meaning, I want to discover it.

I can't deny that my brain plays a creative role in how information is figured and framed. And how I frame my delusions, or whose framing I listen to, will shape the relevance of these experiences and how I proceed from them. By using the word *delusion,* I've already framed my approach. A delusion is by definition wrong. Having said that, I've gone through different phases in interpreting these extreme headspaces, from seeing them as utter nonsense, to learning a lesson from them, to seeing them as a way to access deeply meaningful information. All three of these assessments have a truth to them. I recognize that even the most seemingly sober of perspectives is filtering/inventive in some way, but we all somehow have a similar yet different view on life. I also know that there is realness outside of what I can grasp, and that there is an unknown part of me that has its own form of poetic answer to offer.

There may be a similar mystery to the information found in dreams. Do dreams tell me universal things about myself and the world or are they that mysterious part of me showing things that are mostly relevant to me? Is there a monolithic truth to this, that is an Answer with a capital A, or does each person find their own way with it, with some parts overlapping with others and some not?

Personally, psychosis has taught me that although I may be absolutely certain about something, when I step back and reflect mindfully, I realize my perspective has a propensity to be wrong and that my truth is not always *the* truth. In this way it's humbling.

Although I've had profound moments in the midst my illness, trying to harness positivity is a dangerous game to play. Reversing the momentum of a psychotic disposition can be difficult due to how much your ego wants to ride the wave of it. You can feel very convinced that your headspace has given you access to greater, deeper truths. Is this truth *found* though, or are we constructing it?

Whether we create an essential truth from a situation, or discover one that was there before our experience of it, is a highly debated issue in philosophy. There is a certain amount of sharedness in life, although each person also seems to have been dealt a different set of cards, a particular context that is unique and outside the scope of comparability and universality.

It's important *how* we know the truth. Can something be filtered/affected *and* truthful? Language that discovers and reveals without influence or filter may be an absurd notion. Maybe our filtering is an important creative act? We need to make connections, build images from our environment, make projections and predictions.

Imagining possible scenarios is a very natural and perhaps defining human ability. But if those images are taken to be true, but proven false—and despite the evidence, you believe them to be true—then that's delusional.

It's important that I not impose an unnatural sureness on things that are subjective. This leaves room for future refinement, and for different people's perspectives—their different positions. It's a beautiful thing in life, how art and language can connect these viewpoints and lessen our isolation (11).

Euphoric connection, a link to the unspeakable. It felt like pure goodness, that the song had been forged for this moment. My moment. Each word had a significance, some supernatural link from the general divine to my specific personhood. Could this be? I'm thinking it might be, though other times I've been certain of my involvement in this, this mystical audio ritual.

Idea or Delusion of Reference

It's hard for me to make sense of these moments. They feel so beautifully real and profound, but intoxicating in that sometimes it feels like they imply I'm a saint.

An idea or delusion of reference is when you experience a sign as referring to you when it isn't. For example, listening to a song and thinking it's being sung directly towards you.

Of course, music has a wonderful ability to connect with a wide variety of people, and so in a sense a song can be about you and not about you at the same time. There's the potential for delusion when you create a personalized narrative between you and the song, where you inject an idea that the artist made the work specifically for you even though the maker intended it broadly. Listening to it "as if" it were about you is different from listening to it "as if it literally is" about you, just like when children "play house" they know it's not real life.

Another example of these reference issues is when quick body movements are extrapolated into being signs for you. Sometimes you don't know what the sign is saying: you just think that it's a sign. But you think there is a meaning that is relevant or refers to you.

The difference between an idea of reference and a delusion of reference is that an idea is something that your mind suggests but that you don't believe fully. You see a sign, and think, That's strange, it seems like that's for me. A delusion is when you see the sign and think, That sign *is* for me. But it isn't (12).

The goal should be treating the tendency towards ideas of reference before they become delusions. If there were less stigma about these health issues, people would be more willing to get help before things got worse and the ideas became more rigid. I've been lucky in that a lot of what I've experienced has felt like suggested narratives or signs and haven't led to beliefs written in stone. I'm at a point in my recovery where I get strange suggestions, but am able to disregard them quickly, whereas when I was in the hospital I had a hard time avoiding full commitment to my unrealistic intuitions.

Apart from medication, there are other ways to combat these misrepresentations of stimulus, and here are some that involve critical thinking of some sort (13):

- Stepping back from your thoughts and evaluating them. Thinking about thinking. Meta-thinking. Observing our thoughts is also a part of a meditation technique called mindfulness. In this philosophy, we are what's left when our thoughts are gone. You learn that you are separate from your thoughts and can observe them. It isn't about emptying your mind necessarily, but watching your thoughts as if they were floating along a river. You do your best to stay in the present moment; if you stray, just gently bring your attention back to the breath. The most important part is to try to do this all without judgment. Once we've observed, we can select a thought to examine and then evaluate the evidence as to whether it's true or not. Or we can check in with someone or imagine what someone else might say about this thought.

- Creating a percentage system to give you a more realistic perspective. What other options are there apart from this belief? At first I may think that there's a 100% chance something is true, but if I start to introduce other possibilities, that certainty changes. Let's say I think an option B is 20% likely to happen, option C 25%, option D 30%, and option E 15%. By this logic, that leaves only a 10% chance that my initial belief is correct! The point is to be critical and rational, and to try to find the most likely explanation. What other possible explanations could there be (14)?

These methods are most effective when the belief in question is closer to being an idea of reference rather than a delusion of reference. I try to maintain a healthy amount of doubt in all my beliefs. Who knows what the future may bring that will change my perspective? I reserve the right to change my mind. When I think I'm crazy, I think again (15).

Spiritual/Psychotic

Both psychotic episodes and spiritual visions are certainly ways of seeing the world that differ from "ordinary" views. But whether there is any worth or value in these lines of sight is a controversial issue.

Indigenous people have members of their community who exhibit what may seem to be psychotic-like symptoms, but they aren't treated by their community in the same way that mainstream psychiatry might treat them. Outside of western medicine, these experiences are framed very differently, and as an important insight into the spiritual realm. They aren't just meaningless noise or nonsense: these are visions of a truth deeper than everyday mundanity.

On the other hand, when we say something is psychotic, we are by definition calling it a dysfunction. The brain is not working right (normatively?). One popular hypothesis is that there is a toxic abundance of the dopamine neurotransmitter (16). However, the experience, instead of being hyperreal, may be exactly the opposite. The descriptions of these experiences aren't right or wrong, necessarily—they're unfalsifiable. All subjective experiences lack the criteria to be proved one way or the other. What's normative or pathological, what's true and untrue, is dictated by both the person and the framework or community they subscribe to.

My own experiences of psychosis has entailed me being artificially disconnected from reality and not rooted more deeply into it. It may still be a valid way to view the world, but it is a hellish one. I've thought of myself as disgustingly *other,* like a foreign entity the whole universe was trying to expel. Or so highly elevated above everyone else, as if the natural order was one where the world was engrossed and fascinated with my every move. To me, these distortions are psychotic, unlike a "vision," which is something that provides a clarity that is confirmed by other lenses, other views. Perhaps there is a continuity between past and present perspectives, between what I and others have experienced. This sharedness may take time to be realized as truth.

With spiritual matters, I feel a sense of connection, and have had moments that are ineffable and to me indisputably grand. I have felt sublimely integrated, both submitted and active in the fact that I am not God, but with God.

Because of my lived experience, I'm wary of people romanticizing what I see as an illness as something to embrace and follow in order to find truth. I recognize that everyone is different, but most benefits I've gained as I've experienced psychosis have not been *direct* ones but have served as a means to an end—an awfulness that shakes me to the core, or motivates me to find a method of avoidance.

One of the harder things in life for me to reconcile is when there are these "means to an end" experiences, an immediate bad thing or dysfunction for an ultimate good. Is this unavoidable? To quote Groucho Marx, "Blessed are the cracked for they let in the light" (17). If that's the case, what does it mean to find greater meaning through dysfunction?

I suppose how we frame things dictates their identities, so if there is an ultimate positive, we may not be right to say that what facilitated it is completely dysfunctional.

Can something be bad for the body but good for the mind? Is there a material dysfunction to facilitate spiritual experience?

I can study these things all I want, though at the end of the day my strength comes from speaking from my own experience. I can say for myself what is and isn't spiritual or dysfunctional, but to claim these things for others would be overstepping my place, wrongly imposing my lens, my view, and my framework onto others. Like every Venn diagram, there is sharedness and then uniqueness on both sides with every combination of humans.

There are lots of examples in spiritual traditions of people starving themselves (literally and metaphorically) to experience a divinity. "The flesh," so to speak, is something that is seen to be a worldly mechanism that is to be overcome with discipline and prayer (18). I know for myself though that I'm at my healthiest when both my mind *and* body are well, and for me that means striving for truth in connectedness, and in avoiding the bodily turmoil that leads to those headspaces that have elevated me above and degraded me below our shared reality.

For me, spirituality connects us to the divine, and psychosis takes us away from it. If they both involve the same process in the brain, it goes to show how mysterious we really are.

Sureness

When I was younger, I was convinced there was something mystical about triadic systems. Things like induction, deduction, and abduction. Also, thesis, antithesis, synthesis (19), plus a myriad of other triadic arrangements. Imaginary/symbolic/real (20) or construct/deconstruct/reconstruct, etc. If you're interested in a further exploration of this, check out my Figuring Frames project (21). I'm still quite convinced that there is something sacred about 3's, but I recognize that may be because of my Christian background.

That may explain why in one way, though there are other ways to look at it. All things have different levels or areas of meaning that apply to them. Meanings for their use, meanings for their purpose, immediate and proposed ultimate meanings, etc. I've learned that I never know what new angle or perspective could be found—I never know what the other ways to look at it are—and so I find it important to leave room for potential new information. The information itself is important, but so is *how* that information is found, what tools we use to discover. If we consider how those tools figure and frame, filter and reveal, we can try to compensate for their biases in order to get closer to the truth of the matter.

When I'm delusional I lose my openness and become sure about things where sureness is unrealistic and inappropriate considering the tools I'm using. Things become set in stone when they shouldn't be. I choose one perception as the essential one when such a choice is unwarranted.

We can only ever speak from our own perspective, but through the wonders of language and art, we can empathize with other viewpoints and integrate complementary meanings into that perspective, or consider how someone's conflicting information affects the validity of our own. This diversity of angles helps us form a picture where multiple perspectives coexist, and is important to helping us develop accurate beliefs. As someone who struggles with psychosis, I know that it's really important to be skeptical about the thoughts that pop into my head. Dealing with psychosis has made me realize how beneficial it can be to thoroughly analyze my thoughts before forming beliefs from them.

There are of course areas where a certain sureness is appropriate, like in the world of the senses where things can be tested and verified—though it's worth remembering that even those matters are eventually subjectively mediated. Still, the spectrum between the subjective and the objective exists, and we can't invoke the same verification process for subjective matters as we do for the objective. We would need a God's eye view to fully grasp the ultimate of things. So, since we don't have precise tools for the subjective, it's important to be open in our interpretations. If we are inflexible there is no room for growth. The more open we are, the more available we are for refinement, even of the truths we already believe.

When we write poetry, we speculate, we wonder. We write our visions on the page, but know they are elaborations or new ways of trying to explain topics and subject matter that are hard to verbalize. Although a poem may relate to real things we're grappling with, we know it isn't gospel. It's made up, it's fictional, and although sometimes fiction may seem more real in a strange way, in fact it's *one* perspective, not *the* perspective. We're speculating.

We paint a painting, not a diagram. A diagram explains and tells us what something is, or what the parts are. It is literal, useful, objective. A painting is harder to put into words, and so is hard to explain with words. A painting has an openness that a diagram doesn't. A painting doesn't have to be useful or precise. It doesn't tell you what to believe; it makes suggestions. It presents something that makes you see or feel a certain way, or makes you imagine how things could be. It's allowed to escape usefulness. For me I've found it best to keep the subjective beliefs I attach to thoughts as paintings and not as diagrams, so to speak. There's an openness I find appropriate, to have space for new perspectives or to refine existing ones.

You may find it appropriate to create diagrams for the beyond and divine. Perhaps by embracing the Trinity developed later in Christianity, or the Chakra system within the Tantric tradition. Personally, I oscillate between believing we can and can't know about God and other things which we can't observe. We all have reasons for our beliefs, based on our individual lived experiences. And although I avoid sureness myself, due to having experienced the unreliable though intoxicating nature of delusional perception, I respect the fact that strong faith and belief can be perfectly healthy for others. However, I often have a hard time fully trusting the tools I have available to approach and dissect these big issues, and so I live with the vulnerability of openness. I think this helps facilitate new learning and growth by holding conceptual space for other views.

There is one ethical claim I am stubbornly connected to, and that is the belief that we should aim to decrease suffering in immediate and ultimate ways. That said, sometimes immediate suffering is necessary to avoid a more ultimate one, and predicting which actions are appropriate to alleviate future pain can be difficult. The ultimate perspective is always a work in progress, but we should still do our best to project future possibilities, even though reality might disrupt our expectations.

The suffering we experience in our minds often comes from being isolated or disconnected, either from our communities or from ourselves. So my goal is to integrate myself further with myself and with my community, to imagine and work through possibilities. The variables may be elusive, as matters of mind and mental health are slippery subjects. Perhaps someday sureness about these phenomena will be possible, and there will be enough sameness to connect our perspectives and form a system as elegant and useful as our clocks are for time.

Delusions of Grandeur (The Saint)

In an immediate sense, a delusion of grandeur is incredibly intoxicating. You're artificially heightened in the world. Your art has special powers or you're talking to God.

The most stubborn delusions to conquer are the ones that are unfalsifiable or can't be easily proven wrong, and a lot of subjective experience falls into that category—like art's merit. For me, making art is a mystical activity, not as a part of any religious tradition, but as a way for me to communicate with and integrate my unconscious self. Experiencing the unconscious is, in a way, experiencing a mystery. I believe that this mystery dwells within me, and paradoxically is and is not me (22). The art process helps me connect to something "bigger" than my conscious self, and this decreases the isolation I feel.

This may sound strange, but a lot of beliefs seem strange. I think everyone has their own journey figuring out their own belief framework. If we elevate ours to certainty, we degrade and in a sense dehumanize others. I keep my beliefs as possibilities, as being based on one perspective, recognizing that other people have different perspectives. The dangerous consequence of prioritizing our own view as the essential one is that it establishes the unfounded claim that there is one right way to live, and conveniently that way is ours.

Of course there is some irony at play here, with me telling you what I think is the right way to handle belief. This is my perspective, which is decidedly malleable to future perspectives that art and language may help me integrate.

When I'm delusional, I believe that my art is sacred to everyone and I'm certain of it. When I'm grounded, the art is still sacred, but I don't expect everyone to believe the same thing. It's both shared and isolated, in that there are others who hold similar ideas, and people who will disagree. They're welcome to disagree: I don't exactly have evidence to support my position.

It seems like some beliefs are more obviously delusional than others. A belief that tells you the whole world is watching your every move because of your divinely appointed abilities may feel like gospel when you're experiencing it. I know this from experience, which elevates me away from reality. It embarrasses me to admit that I've actually held that condescending belief, but I share it with you in case someone who is reading this can relate. There's no shame in having been delusional, but delusions are to be avoided, because of the suffering, namely the isolation, they entail.

The first psychosis I had that required hospitalization happened while I was working on a record (23). For the album art I intended to let myself go completely. I suppose I chose that, but I didn't know the implications at the time. It was an awesome thing to experience, making that art, but it would prove difficult to "put myself back together" after letting go so completely. In truth, I didn't even get "good" art out of it, in that the art wasn't nearly as impactful as I thought it would be while making it. And I had wanted impact.

Every mark felt so profound, the symbols pointing to some hidden truth that I was uncovering. It felt like a sacred exercise that I was destined to partake in. To me this wasn't simply good art, it was art that had universal significance, more of a discovery than a creation, in that it pointed to deep sublime truth that I was uncovering. When we're delusional, we think we're making something brilliant, but in a shared reality it's often less impressive, less universal than we think it is. We see connections while we're making it that the viewer and our future self may not perceive later. That's not to say that the work isn't valuable as a sort of diary, or isn't relevant to ourselves as a means to process our thoughts. The art process doesn't always need an object at the end of it to be worthwhile.

Sometimes making things without considering how they're received may ironically create something that others relate to more. A lot of art doesn't make any sense, and I think there's something very beautiful about that in a world fixated on the understandable. Our nonsense is perfectly valuable on its own. It reflects a truth of this world, that part which isn't rational. It's wild.

But we can't expect what we experience to be shared in the same way by others, who are seeing the work without our internal dialogue. If you expect it to connect, and it doesn't—be kind to yourself. Maybe you're new at this. Art making is a muscle, and it takes time to strengthen it. In my experience, when I'm delusional, drunk, etc., I'm not concerned about palatability, and I can exhibit a certain arrogance. It's strange, because it feels so great while doing it: I'm convinced it's exceptional. I've done a lot of writing that felt like it was going to change the world, only to look back on it and think, *Who is this grandiose, pretentious fool?*

Those projects, however, were stepping stones for me to get to where my voice is now. Because it was early in the process, my content wasn't quite palatable and was greatly obscured by my ego. Palatability isn't necessary with creative endeavours, but don't expect a piece to resonate well when a lot of its content lives only in your brain. It's the same thing with delusions. You experience them up close, whereas the world only hears your words and sees your behaviour. With art it's important that you find a process that you enjoy and that you remain patient. It takes time to develop and integrate your inner world into something well communicated to the outer one.

Having said all this, art can leave us mystified and still be worthwhile. It all depends on what you're intending to do. Maybe isolating your audience creates a tension that you find appropriate? Maybe you intend to be unaware of your intentions? Or maybe your audience is a select group of people and not the general public? Maybe it's about finding a balance, where you suggest something that the viewer themself creates meaning from? Laying things out fully turns the work into a technical manual or an essay, but not giving any clues means the work is inaccessible noise.

It is an intoxicating feeling to dance with your mind, connections flying through as dialogue is formed and elaborated. But in an ultimate sense, having a delusion of grandeur is demoralizing. First you felt "blessed by God," only now you're framed as psychotic. Coming down from this is really hard, and is partly why I've clung to certain delusions. Being wrong was just too hard to bear, much like embracing the fact that we have the ability to choose can be excruciating too. With a delusion of grandeur, it can be incredibly painful to come "back to earth," where we live in a culture where humility is expected. You feel as though you're a monster. So I swing too far the other way, into self-hatred and depression. Finding that healthy level of self-esteem afterwards can be difficult, when my sickness imposes extreme beliefs in both directions.

It's only a matter of time. They despise me. I've made the wrong move and now there's no getting away from it, away from this mess I made. I can see in the subtle movements of their faces that they are offended by my existence.

Paranoia (The Villain)

Worrying about our safety is useful, as it can help protect us from threats. Our minds may prefer to over-suggest, because if we're wrong the stakes are lower than if we under-speculate. When we're paranoid though, our suggestions are outlandish.

Paranoia is a type of illusion/delusion in that it is thinking something that isn't true. It's speculating in a way that makes us out to be more of a villain than we actually are. It can be terrifying to be paranoid, and when people are scared, they can be erratic. These experiences are real to the person experiencing them, so it also makes sense how they could be traumatic.

It's very uncomfortable to experience these beliefs. There is a lot of fear, a lot of uncertainty. You're worried about further suffering, sometimes worried that your loved ones might suffer too. I'm not sure if these sorts of beliefs are there to make us change our behaviour in some way, but it's very hard to convince me that my belief isn't the case if it's delusional. I can step back and tell myself that what I believe isn't true, but still feel it and experience it to be true. How strange the mind is, with its layers that relay and filter inwardly and outwardly, recursively.

There are a few reasons why it's hard to bring someone back to earth when they're experiencing paranoia. The foremost, I think, is that the person trying to reason with you can be wrongly perceived as an enemy. There's the right person saying the wrong thing, but also the right words coming from someone we don't trust. When I'm psychotic I'm not sure whose "team" people are on, or whose team people think *I'm* on.

I've heard that the best way to help someone who is in the middle of a delusion is to ask questions, trying to gain their trust (24). Trust is a basis for understanding. Don't agree with what they're saying but try not to disagree either. Ask questions so that the person has a chance to see flaws in their logic, so that they can have the chance to change their own minds. Whatever you do, you want it to be accessible to the individual experiencing the delusion. Aim to connect them back to the sensory/objective realm, because often when you're delusional you're fixated on the conceptual/subjective side of life. Making art may be helpful, or simply going for a walk. Grounding myself in these ways has been very helpful.

For me, the most effective way to come back to reality was with antipsychotic medication. So, getting help from healthcare professionals was important. I had thought medication was poison before though, and in that case I was sick enough to be admitted to a psychiatric ward against my will. This is not a great option but is preferable when we become a danger to ourselves or others. I wasn't violent towards others, but was on the verge of suicide. Thankfully with medication I gradually integrated back into the shared real. Antipsychotics have some significant side-effects, and aren't a viable option for everyone, but their development has moved mental healthcare dramatically forward, in my opinion. At least, they have been successful for me.

Most importantly, when I'm experiencing paranoia, I need to feel safe again. To return to that middle ground. Not to think of myself as some sort of angel or demon, but to remember that I'm that messy mix of good and bad which is human.

Delusion or Intuition?

A delusion is by definition false, and intuition is simply a suggestion, which may be either wrong or right. So a delusion is an intuition that has been wrongly decided upon.

Some dreams are more relevant or true to our life than others. The same goes for intuitions. Our intuitions are more easily abandoned, as we can say "my intuition was off with that one." Whereas a delusion is typically something you still believe even when shown evidence to the contrary.

With a few practical cognitive behavioural techniques, we can determine whether a thought is an intuition or an intuition that's become delusional. First and foremost, we need to meta-think. By that I mean we need to think about our thinking, to step back and examine a thought. Is there evidence for this thought? What would someone else say about my belief if I told them? What other options could it be?

Another helpful way is to write something down, to question it, to be critical of it. Externalize it. Allow yourself to be confronted by it. If it's something you can't be sure one way or another about, honour that. Be comfortable with it being a maybe, and avoid cementing the voice that says, "It's this, and only this."

I feel like the best intuition comes in multitudes, that is, we produce multiple options to choose from. Could be this, could be that. Let's compare them. What do I think? But I don't have to do this all the time. Sometimes it's important to be passive, stand beside the river and just watch my thoughts pass by.

An Undefined View

If you're like me and have experienced abnormal headspaces, you may think of them as being filled with nonsense, or alternatively with content that is worth exploring further. For me some of what I've experienced while psychotic has felt profound, either in the direct experience of it or in the reflection about it afterwards. And on the other side of things, where there's paranoia, the fear has given me insight into trauma, made me feel worthless and so revoltingly other.

Either way, these views are a part of my story whose ultimate relevance I am decidedly uncertain of. It is hard to reconcile that an underlying condition could produce such dramatically different results, equal only in how extreme they are. I don't think we have the language to respectfully and fully relay the nuances of such bizarre experiences. They are not simply good/normal or bad/pathological; they are ways of seeing the world, of living in the world. Whatever you call them, they're part of the human experience. And the brain chemistry that builds a view for me to embrace may be something that I find extremely negative and to be avoided. An experience for you may evoke a headspace that you feel is privileged, though for me it could evoke a view that is a burden to bear. If your views aren't getting in the way of how you want to live your life, and you're not harming others, then who am I to say you should avoid them? I just find it strange to call something that's positive *psychotic*, when *psychotic* as a word connotes wrongness and abnormality. Do we refine what we mean when we say that word, or do we need a new word altogether? I'm not sure.

I want a connectedness in my own mental health and spirituality that is more sober than intoxicating, more grounding than artificially heightened.

For me there's delusion in claiming to know the unknowable, in deeming the unreal real. When I'm delusional, I make answers that abandon the vulnerability of openness. This is an issue because it disregards the space I should keep for future perspectives. It may escape me sometimes, but there is a peace to be found in submitting to the fact that we're limited by our immediate and particular views, and so shouldn't be expected to hold ultimate and universal answers for all-encompassing questions.

Romanticization of the Tortured Artist

We don't want to demonize illness, but we should be equally careful not to romanticize it either. In my experience, I may *feel* most creative in bouts of mania and/or psychosis, but it's when I'm sober and well that I produce my best work.

It's worth thinking about how immediate bads can be for an ultimate good. We have things we go through in life that are awful, but we learn lessons from them. Something bad is reinterpreted to be good by how we frame it. Horrible things are mitigated into things not so horrible. This is one of the hardest things about life to reconcile. The pain of something when it's being experienced may not be positive, but ultimately it may serve as inspiration or as source material for art, or as an experience that teaches us something. A means to an end. Or sometimes instead of making the best out of bad situations, an artist portrays bad situations as warnings for the future.

The pain I've experienced from my illness has motivated me to create by giving me problems to solve. I create visual art where I brainstorm with text to make sense of the world, sometimes to review the judgments I've attached to memories to get to a more realistic perspective. This is one approach to art making, but I think that artists can be inspired by all sorts of things. Working from real suffering, representing the realness of our human condition, is important and admirable, but should be done from suffering that is unavoidable—either because it's stubbornly in the present or because it's now cemented as past.

Sacrificing ourselves in an immediate sense for some ultimate or eventual good is a dangerous game to play. I know for myself that I've justified bad decisions because I thought I was on the path to a great work of art, or because I thought I was embodying some character that I thought was admirable. In reality though, the positivity of that character is only viable in the imaginary realm. The reality of the tortured artist is dark and lonely and without the prestige and romance I imagine. There is only sad suffering when I live it in the flesh.

Psychiatric Hospitals

There is both a dark side and a bright side to spending time in one of these hospitals. I had some dark moments and memories that I recorded:

I felt like a wounded animal cowered on the floor. My head against your heart, reaching for the safety of its rhythm. The staff tore me away and held me with leather to a bed; stillness had never felt so chaotic.

There is no shortage of that sort of memory for me from that time. If I had to choose two words from the dark vantage point to explain a psych ward, they would be *fragmented* and *disconnected.* Each person in there is struggling with their own blend of disconnection from reality, be it depression or psychosis. Everyone has some distortion they are dealing with. This can make for a chaotic environment, as these skewed perspectives are bound to clash, both internally and in people's dealings with each other, staff included.

Part of improving my health was learning to trust the doctors and nursing staff. It's a hard thing to do when you're in a new and strange environment and you're not sure who is on your side. Meetings with your doctor can feel cold and sterile, and so I think it would benefit people to have trained peer support workers there to try to bridge the hierarchy between doctor and patient. It's a vulnerable place to be, and to commit to working with the system can be difficult when there aren't people present who have been in your shoes. The whole thing feels dystopian. Other patients there might be anti-psychiatry or with their own hesitations, and try to convince you not to trust the people who are trying to help you. The system isn't perfect, and some doctors are certainly better than others, but we have to do what we can with what we have available.

It can be an emotional battle to survive the psych ward environment and the environment of your own mind. It can feel like a maze, with each moment something new to endure. For me, I was dealing with paranoia and delusions of grandeur, so there was always some new plot to figure out or next move to overanalyze. There are so many characters in the place, so many variables to reckon with. Being there felt overwhelming and induced panic. I, as a relatively large person, was generally terrified. I can't imagine what it would be like for someone more physically vulnerable.

For a close friend or family member, I can imagine it is its own sort of hell, seeing your loved one in such a damaged state and in such a strange environment. I've had family members stop visiting me. They either were trying to prove a point or couldn't handle it.

When people are sick, they can be pretty intense. I am very sensitive to people's emotional energy, and I found talking to certain people to be very dark and unsettling. You could tell some of the staff were burnt out and that was hard to deal with too. Making it through the three month-long periods I spent there was one of the hardest things I've ever had to do. I still have a difficult time reconciling those experiences. It was traumatic, though I know it could have been even more traumatic if I had been out in the real world.

The bright side ...

Nothing I've said changes the fact that I am very *thankful* these places exist. If it weren't for antipsychotic medication and the safety of the psych ward, I would probably be dead. There was a lot of suffering, but there could have been a lot more.

So, this disconnect from the real world was also a positive thing. I was monitored and had limited stimulation to give my brain time to heal. However, interactions with other patients were sometimes overly stimulating, but being there was a much lesser evil than being left to my own devices. I was being dealt with by professionals, so my family and friends didn't have to shoulder that burden. As I recovered I became more comfortable and developed a routine. I met some very kind people, and in retrospect I'm pretty damn proud that I endured my insanity. There are big issues to tackle regarding psych wards. Having trained peer support workers present would be beneficial. We need to improve the conditions in these units, not get rid of them. And maybe most importantly, help people before things get bad enough for hospitalization.

Doctors

A good doctor is a good detective. They do their best to connect the right actions to the right outcomes, and work with you to find solutions to the problems they find. They can sense when you're struggling to describe an experience, and understand that their understanding of what certain words mean might be different than what your understanding of them is. You may describe something as mania, when it is actually psychosis. Language matters.

A good doctor is someone who helps you realize the flaws in your logic without being judgmental or condescending.

A good doctor stays up to date. They're aware of the current dialogue surrounding your issues, of the history you have as a patient, as well as the contemporary literature available.

A good doctor isn't jaded. They're still hopeful and still care.

A good doctor supports you through the grounding process.

A good doctor makes you feel safe.

Peer Support

In 2018 I was trained by the Canadian Mental Health Association as a peer support worker. For me, peer support is all about utilizing lived experience.

When I was in peer support training, we would sit in a circle and discuss the tenets/philosophy of peer support, as well as what being in recovery and being a peer support worker mean. There was one particular concept I had a hard time accepting.

I wasn't in the greatest of headspaces at that time, and remember writing strange grandiose reflections in my journal that my mentor would review. Musings about free will that were a scattered mix of poetry and self-help sermons. Although embarrassing, it was an important step for me to take. I've always had a hard time writing, as until that point I'd been too critical to keep words on the page with these topics.

One of the themes I started writing about after that was free will. The idea of "self-determination" was hard for me to accept—the idea that we all have the power to change our situation. That we have free will. I find this relates to mental health in a strong, albeit a possibly controversial way.

At the time I was very skeptical that we had any sort of free will. I believed that life was imposed on us. I didn't choose to be born, because I would have had to already be born in order to choose. I thought that in life we have the illusion of choice and nothing more. Are we choosing if there aren't any viable alternatives to what we're choosing? If we are dealt a bad hand, how can we be expected to play well? Is it not completely out of my control as to what's been deemed "well"? During peer school I was beginning to wrestle with these issues outside of my head and on the page. It's a process I continue to this day, to try to make sense of these big issues.

I find it really helpful to externalize our thoughts and ideas, and work through them in a tangible way like through writing. There's a certain clarity that comes from having something outside of ourselves to reflect with, to mould and react to. It can be an uncomfortable process, as we're confronted with what we might not be aware of, but I find it very rewarding and good for my mental health.

As for mental health, I think that believing in choice is a double-edged sword. If we say we have a choice and that there is a division between good and bad choices, we must take responsibility for the bad choices that we've made, that we had control over. This can be really painful. But on the flip side, if we say we have a choice, we have a way out of our situation in that we admit we have the ability to make choices that we want for ourselves and others. We're empowered.

As for what is and isn't out of your control, that's for you to decide. It can be really harmful when people tell us that something is in our control when it isn't. Peer support is all about valuing the perspective of the person living with what's being talked about, and recognizing that each of us knows ourself best in determining what is and isn't feasible to change or not change. As friends and family members we can come alongside people and talk through potential possibilities, but it's important to recognize the fact that it's up to the person themself to live their life how they can.

When I started writing about free will, I was grappling with a friend's suicide. I didn't want it to be, in any way, his fault that he didn't pull himself out of his misery. I wasn't mad at him; I was mad at the world for allowing or creating such disparity in mental anguish. As for myself, I didn't want to face the pain I'd been handed, and hadn't come to terms with the decisions I had made that had helped lead to that pain. I was unsure about my future, unsure I deserved a decent one.

Peer support taught me that recovery is about self-acceptance and allowing yourself to dream. Daring to want something out of our lives. If I had to describe peer support quickly, I would call it sharing lived experience to instill hope.

Peer support helped me realize I was not alone in this fight, and that other people faced similar struggles of being held back by their past with health troubles. I learned to focus on what I can control. To focus on what was strong, not what was wrong. This provided the perspective I needed to move forward in my life. I may not be able to control a lot of things, but I can control how I react, how I interpret what comes towards me.

It's way easier said than done, but focusing on the future and learning to be realistic with the past is a fantastic form of self-care. I learned that recovery is a process, not a destination. That I would face some serious ups and downs throughout life that others wouldn't have to endure, but that was o.k. because maybe the highs I have that they don't would make up for it.

I've diminished myself with all sorts of soft suicidal acts. Smoking, self-harm, starving during the day. I've made decisions that indicate how I don't feel worthy to be taken care of. This has negatively affected me, but also the communities I belong to. They've cared more about me than I have for myself. But who always does what's best for themself? I suppose there's a spectrum.

Suicide

This is a topic I am hesitant to write about, because I really don't want to write something that would lead to more suffering. How we write about suicide matters, although it's important we feel comfortable talking and expressing where we're at with it so that we feel less alone. The main issue, I think, with how we communicate about suicide is that we don't want to condone the act, but we don't want to blame a person for doing it either.

I have heard that suicide doesn't end the suffering, it just passes it on to other people. Isn't this blaming the ill? This view is frustrating, because a part of me is sympathetic to it. The suffering after a suicide is impossibly immense for the loved ones still here. As for the person who ends their life, I suppose we all have our beliefs. Personally, I'd be wary of anyone claiming absolutes about what happens after death: they might be trying to sell you something. I do know that their suffering in this life is over, and if there is nothing after death, then there is neither suffering nor joy. Nothing is characterless.

The suffering in this life is not nothing, and some people have impossible amounts of it imposed on them. The battle is fought valiantly, but the hero leaves us sometimes. Mental illness is illness, just like cancer is. You don't blame someone for suffering from cancer, do you? But if this analogy were completely accurate, there wouldn't be a delineation between mental and physical health. Or are they the same? If they are the same, what of euthanasia? These are hard issues.

I believe there's a difference between physical and mental health, and that difference is in the fact we have a dimension to ourselves that chooses. We are beings who deal with meaning, and meaning isn't material.

In dealing with mental health, am I really choosing if I'm not aware of the ultimate implications of my actions? Is it a choice if there isn't freedom to choose otherwise? We have to be careful in saying there is no choice, because we don't want to doom people to an outcome, and we don't want to condone decisions that lead to suffering. People who are ill make decisions they wouldn't necessarily make if they had access to a more diverse picture. Our perspective is clouded by illness and positions that aren't integral to us.

I wish I could bring back my friends who struggled valiantly, but ultimately were overcome by their mental illness. There are things I would have done differently, choices I wish I didn't make. But we can't impose today's knowledge on yesterday's decisions. I know for myself that in my darkest times there have been a few things that have kept me from taking my own life. Some of them may seem too dark to say, but I'll say them anyway.

A high percentage of suicide attempts are unsuccessful (25). To me the thought of being physically as well as mentally crippled by an unsuccessful attempt has played a part in keeping me here. Another thing is that life can be hellish in the moment, but you don't know what improvements tomorrow may bring. All moods and feelings are temporary (even the good ones, unfortunately). What has helped me the most is understanding my purpose. I need purpose. With purpose, be it handed down or chosen, we can withstand almost anything. "He who has a why to live for can bear almost any how," as Nietzsche said (26).

So, with my beliefs in mind, I carry on. When an hour of this life seems too much to bear, I take it minute by minute, and when that is too much, I take it second by second, trying to keep in mind that the next second could be a better one.

What's Causing What

There is a vast variety of proposed causes for psychosis. Concussions, physical sickness like lupus, brain injury, sleep deprivation, trauma, drugs and alcohol, major depressive disorder, etc. These are a few causes that along with genetic factors can play a role in someone developing psychosis (27).

Before my first hospitalization, I wasn't sleeping, was severely stressed due to school and my performance schedule as a musician, was dealing with deaths in my close circle, and was consuming high-THC cannabis. My resiliency was at an all-time low.

A few words about cannabis ... Am I mentally ill because I smoked cannabis, or did I smoke cannabis because of trauma or pre-existing mental illness and was dealing with it by self-medicating in some way? I've mentioned my delusion when I was 12 years old, but would that have been an isolated incident if it weren't for my cannabis use?

It's an important question to me, whether cannabis was or wasn't a factor. Did it create my mental health issues, or did it activate something that was dormant. A propensity. Maybe it didn't play a causal role at all, and there were other factors responsible, such as sleep deprivation, extreme emotional turmoil, and overall poor self-care? Did these all play some part in the breakdown? It's likely it was a combination of factors. Everything changes the brain. Isolating variables well enough to determine what's causal or correlated is difficult.

I do know though that not everyone who smokes weed is going to get sick, just like not everyone who is sleep deprived and stressed for a month is going to get sick either. Everyone has their own breaking point, and some people's tolerance is lower than others'. I know now that cannabis may feel wonderful in an immediate sense, though ultimately it's likely not doing me much good. But even if it isn't doing any harm, what are the positives? Writing down pros and cons lists has been helpful for me to see whether activities are worth my while. Of course, it's not a simple case of the larger number on one side of the list beating out the number on the other side. Variables are not necessarily equivalent, and one may be extremely relevant and important, while another may be relatively minor.

When I was first hospitalized, there was the perfect storm I mentioned above. The doctors focused on the drug use and that made things more difficult for me. Afterwards, I felt the shame of my choices with self-medication and wanted to know if I had caused this whole mess. The issue with focusing too much on social causes is that we risk neglecting the biological ones. We can't control our genetics, whereas our ability to control social factors is up for debate. Getting fixated on what ultimately caused the breakdown wasn't important though. What was important was that I looked to the future and worked to improve in the areas I could control.

I was born with a vulnerability towards psychosis and other mental health issues. I can't control my genetics, or other deaths that I will inevitably have to endure, though I can control how I take care of myself and what I put into my body. I can if I care. If I want to be well. Before the psychosis I was living a certain way because of anxiety and depression issues. And then after the psychosis I fell into a deep depression, like so many people do. Part of what was sick with me was that I didn't want to get well. I felt great shame for what had become of my story. I hated myself, so why would I put effort into me?

Trauma can lead to self-medication and self-medication can help activate a psychosis. This leads to more trauma, which can lead to more self-medication. For me, what broke this cycle was not caring about myself more, but becoming more aware of how other people were suffering because of my illness. I wanted to die, but couldn't take my own life. It would have been too hard on the people around me. I was in this awful in-between of wanting out of my life, but being stuck in it.

It takes a long time to fix these things. In truth, I'm still working on it. But I now consider myself in recovery, because I'm doing my best to take better care of myself, for myself and others. Some days I fall back into old patterns, but I try not to focus on that, I try to focus on where I want to go. I know that if I don't suffer in small ways now, I or others will suffer more in the future. Sometimes it's worth it to suffer. Life is strange but worth it. There's meaning here, whether we discover it or create it.

Happening to and by Us

There are both genetic and social factors which enable and facilitate psychosis. Not everyone who has trauma will become psychotic, and not everyone who has the potential for psychosis will live it.

Throughout history, certain positions on this issue have led to a gross mistreatment of the mentally ill. The past is filled with dark ideas that deem the sick as having lives not worth living. Some have said we're incurable and that it's appropriate to sterilize us to prevent future generations of deviance and dysfunction (28). On one hand there has been this justification that care or recovery is hopeless due to biologically determined factors, and on the other toxic hand there has been the supernatural explanations that require the mentally ill to require some form of exorcism due to actions they made that caused their psychosis. It's toxic to place responsibility for the illness solely on the person who's ill, by saying that only their decisions led them to being sick. It's also toxic to say that recovery isn't possible because we're just "programmed" this way.

Figuring out what's in and out of our control can be a difficult skill to learn. I know there've been traumatic moments in my life that I've wrongly blamed myself for, thinking I had control when I really didn't. It's healing to rethink yourself away from being some villain who chose wrong. Many things in life we don't choose, and often our choice is minimized because we don't realize the more ultimate implications of our choices when we make them. Having said that, it's also important for me to retain the power to overcome my situations, not to be a total victim of circumstance. We don't choose our genetics, and we don't choose the trauma that happens to us, but we do choose how we respond.

Recovery looks different for everyone, and our limitations vary and are best defined by the person experiencing them. I do my best not to subscribe to the narrative that I am "fundamentally broken" and try to embrace the idea that although I may be different than many others, I'm not pathological: I'm neurodivergent.

If I hadn't been handed down the genes that facilitated my psychosis, I might not have received my creativity, my imagination, my unique view on this world. It's much harder to find a bright side to trauma, and I'm fairly certain the positive aspects of myself are despite and not because of it. All these variables are complicated and hard to isolate from each other. I am who I am because of all of these things that have been handed to me and that I've made happen. Life is a dance between accepting and refusing to accept the stories we are told and are telling ourselves.

Immediate/Ultimate (As It Relates to Addiction)

Immediate and ultimate realities relate to a lot in life, including addiction. I know for myself that I've found the most success by substituting healthy pleasure or relief for unhealthy ones. There is a lot of pain in addiction, and I don't think it makes sense to take away self-medication without replacing it with something good for us, in a more ultimate sense. Self-medicating is still medicating. There is a problem that needs to be solved, which is often some sort of pain or trauma. Also, I've spent too much time focusing on what not to do, what I've done wrong. What about what I *can* do, and what I can do *right?*

I've always had a hard time connecting immediate circumstances with more ultimate ones. When I'm most active in my addiction I ignore how the decisions I'm making in the present will affect future realities.

Drug use which is relieving/positive in an immediate sense can also be responsible for an uncomfortable/negative reality in a more ultimate sense. As an addict, I've needed to get better at empathizing with the future than simply enjoying the present.

The healthier pleasures in life often don't come to us immediately, and require some form of discomfort for eventual satisfaction. Exercise, for example, often feels like a chore, but we feel great when we're finished. I find it helpful to imagine that future feeling as something to work towards. Paradoxically, the motivation to do the activity comes from doing the activity. This may tempt us to tell our struggling friend or family member to just do the activity, but this isn't in fact helpful. They may be stuck in the awful catch-22 of "I need to go for a run to feel better, but I need to feel better to be able to go for a run."

I've found that a way to progress in my recovery is to start small, so, not "just do the activity," but "just do what you can." Maybe it isn't a run you should start with, but five push-ups, and after that you may feel motivated to walk around the block, and in a couple of days you'll go for that run. Reminds me of the book *One Red Paperclip* (29), in which Kyle MacDonald describes starting with a paperclip and trading it for things of increasing value until he eventually had a house.

Perhaps, though, you're in such a dark place that you can't do much of anything. For me, this is where medication and talking things through with a doctor helped point me in a positive direction. I had been taught not to try to "think" my way out of depression or addiction. I had been told that it's behaviour that makes the difference, that changes the brain more dramatically. It can be possible to solve these issues on our own, but there's certainly no shame in asking for help—for a problem we didn't choose to have. Now is when we make those next steps, dealing with the circumstances we are in *this time,* as we did a previous time. The things we were born with are always there now and always with us.

Shame can get in the way of forward momentum. It's a balance between challenging yourself by being ambitious and understanding that we can only move ourselves one step at a time. The unkind criticism we smother ourselves with for not reaching our unrealistic expectations is counterproductive with the disguise of it enhancing productivity. It's much easier to make small positive steps without the weight of shame.

More Thoughts on Addiction

- It can be harmful to delay gratification too much. In the past, peasants would put up with hell, hoping they'd eventually get to heaven. The power dynamics at play between those peasants and the wealthy are harmful. I should strive to be like the Buddha, who walked the middle path between asceticism and indulgence (30)
- My immediate actions may seem productive but can lead to an ultimate suffering, namely for my family
- A healthy pleasure can become a problematic pleasure if I have an unhealthy relationship with it and use it to excess
- It's not going to be one activity that fixes me. I need to find balance in my life
- I need to process and come to terms with trauma, confront the discomfort in a safe place with a safe person
- The story I tell myself about myself will dictate if I think I deserve to be well
- Motivation often follows the activity, not the other way around. This is so strange

Means to an End

Immediate and ultimate realities relate to other things such as our morality (something being immediately bad but ultimately good), eating habits, and climate change. We may accept something that is immediately bad if it leads to something that is ultimately good. The opposite is true as well. We've also become so disconnected from the harsh realities of some of our basic services, for example, that I don't think I'd eat meat if I saw the reality of how it gets to my plate.

Who I Want to Be

I used to wake up in the middle of the night and get flashbacks of being in the hospital when I was sick with appendicitis. I would remember hobbling to the washroom, feeling like I was in some foreign land. The vulnerability of it all was horrible. I'd worry while looking back that I'd end up in a place like that again. I'd worry that the decisions I was making in life were leading me there.

The self-medicating I was doing wouldn't lead me there certainly, but not exercising, drinking excessively, and other ways of being destructive to myself increase the odds of an eventually miserable situation. And yet, I kept doing these things because they felt great in an immediate sense. I'd have moments of sickness where I'd swear to myself that I'd change, though when I was back in a comfortable state I forgot those notions.

I didn't want to be that way. I wanted to be more disciplined, to derive pleasure from healthier activities different from the cheap thrills I'd become accustomed to. I wanted to wake up early in the morning and study philosophy. I wanted to be thriving in my career, to meditate daily and go for walks, to eat less meat. I knew hypothetically I could do this, but how? How could I get there?

Dangerously Close to Advice

Dear Younger John,

Being mentally ill is a horrible struggle. We are bombarded with solutions—from friends, family, and doctors all doing their best to say the right thing. There is a paradox of choice. You did not choose to get ill, but you can improve your situation.

Those two facts can cause a lifetime of tension and need for reconciliation. Ironically, if we were to say that there is no choice at all in life, we would relieve the suffering of guilt; but if we say there is a choice, we will facilitate guilt but have a way out of our situation. It is not this black and white but it can be helpful to think about it that way.

"I have to meditate to feel better, but I have to feel better to want to meditate."

The truth is that *there is* something to fill that hole, or rather to activate positive momentum, but nobody knows what that is. The mistake is to think there is no hope, and that *you* know that, or that *they* know and it's your fault for not being able to do what they tell you. Both parties are trying to figure it out together.

That suggestion to just do an activity is wrong because of its lack of nuance, not because of its basic structure. Doing *anything* is easier to say than to actually do. Who always does what is best for themself?

Still, it's wrong to answer this question with, "oh just do this, or do that." It's the lack of motivation or ability to do these things that needs fixing. However, as I've said previously, sometimes action or activity comes first, and the motivation follows.

A few things to consider trying:

- exercise
- improving your nutrition
- meditation/mindfulness
- Eye Movement Desensitization and Reprocessing (EMDR) therapy (seems to be particularly helpful for trauma victims) (31)
- cognitive behavioural therapy
- various forms of psychotherapy
- narrative therapy
- work as a way to improve self-esteem
- alternative therapy (art/music)

I'm sure there are many more. Hopefully one positive thing leads to another and so on.

Medication is another alternative. One of the great things about medication is that it can kickstart a person into making healthier decisions, or into implicating some of the more "natural" solutions. Downsides and side-effects?

Yes, so it's best to discuss the risks and possible benefits with a doctor.

At the end of the day, it's about finding what works for you. The best solutions are the ones you will actually instigate. We don't get well overnight. Sometimes it's about making small changes that perpetuate into big ones. Ultimately, I would recommend finding a doctor who can help you through this process.

One step at a time and remember to celebrate your successes—no matter how small.

Your Friend,
Older John

Reaching Out

Reaching out for mental health help is a process, and it may take multiple efforts to get the resources that work for you. You might not connect with the first therapist you sit down with, or your family doctor might not listen to you in a way that's helpful. That first pill you try may not work out, but that shouldn't necessarily stop you from trying another. Keep trying things until you find solutions that are relevant. And just because something is easy or hard for you doesn't mean it would be the same for others. Your experience isn't the only way to experience the world. The nature of my choice is different from yours.

Words of Affirmation

You deserve to talk to yourself kindly.
You deserve to inhabit space.
You can forgive yourself for not knowing better at the time.
Not every thought you think is true.
Rethink those toxic thoughts.
You are not your feelings.
You are not your thoughts.
What we are is a mystery.
It's o.k. to let go of things you can't control.
We make clocks, not time.
What you believe someone thinks may not be the case.
You deserve to talk to yourself kindly!
You're not a burden.

Depression

The biggest challenge I face when I'm depressed isn't in finding any particular solution necessarily, but being willing to instigate solutions. When I'm really depressed, I hate myself. Why would I want to fix something I hated? So when someone says "*just* do [insert proposed solution here]," it's not helpful. In a way it's asking me to solve a problem that wouldn't be there if I cared enough to solve it. It's the paradox of "I need to write down my thoughts to feel better, but I need to feel better to be able to write down my thoughts." I can break the cycles, of course, but which cycles are feasible to break can only be decided by me, the person who lives with them.

I Don't Care

Sometimes when I say that I don't care, I really mean that I care too much to risk losing what I might lose if I say that I care. If I don't care about an issue, I'm not invested, and can't be hurt if things turn out differently than how I would have wanted them to.

Intrusive Thoughts

Everyone has strange and awful thoughts they don't want. You don't consciously choose automatic thoughts.

Things That Work for Me (Anxiety/Panic)

- I learned breathing techniques to use in times of panic. One that works really well for me is breathing in for 3 seconds, holding it for 3 seconds, breathing out for 3 seconds, and then repeating (32)
- I learned a *really* good grounding exercise to do when I'm panicking called the "54321." Notice 5 things you see, 4 things you hear, 3 things you smell, 2 thinks you feel, and 1 thing you taste. I'm not sure where this idea originated
- When things are really bad, I've found that putting an icepack on my forehead and leaning into it works really well to calm me down (33)
- I try to remember that every mood, every state of mind, is temporary
- I stand and notice—notice how my feet are connected to the ground

Things That Work for Me (Psychosis)

- Learning my symptom activators. If you're noticing that you're "receiving unnatural signs," take action to reduce them before you become convinced they're real
- Learning openness: you can reserve the right to change your mind
- Avoiding social media. Although I want to broadcast my intuitions, I avoid social media because I know I'll likely regret it later
- Sleep. It is healing and can also serve as a reset
- Medication
- Meditation

Things That Work for Me (Heightened Mood/Mania)

- Listening to music. When I'm manic, I want to run, write, paint, do all sorts of activities that only spur on the mania. It's hard, but I do my best to do calming things, like meditating, limiting stimulation, etc. (easier said than done, like swimming upstream). Sometimes I feel the need to be doing something, but doing relaxing activities at that moment isn't realistic. I've found in those moments that listening to music absorbs my energy in a strange way

Things That Work for Me (In General)

- Doing my best to be kind. When you're kind, people are usually more willing to help you
- Making art. Art is a bridge. An artist translates conceptual objects into exterior sensory ones. Art bridges us with other people as we connect over favourite paintings and favourite songs. It bridges ourselves within ourselves, as the conscious integrates the unconscious mind. Art gives me purpose, as I try to find that perfect image. Art translates beauty. Art creates or points to beauty

Pharmaceutical Medication

I have tried antidepressants, mood stabilizers, and antipsychotics, all in quite a few versions. It's been a process of trial and error to see what would work and wouldn't work. And a sometimes painful process of trial and error. (There are risks to taking these medications, so it's important you and your team are aware of them.)

It took some time, but I found a combination that works. I'm thankful to have had the support of my family and friends throughout this process. It required a great deal of patience from all of us.

I don't feel groggy or foggy now, or sedated in any way. In fact, when I found what worked, I began to feel more myself. More clear. Some describe it as not that they changed, but the whole world changed. Of course, this isn't the case, but it's an interesting commentary on perception. Medication certainly has the potential to be life-changing. It hasn't been a perfect fix, and I often have to tweak amounts or change things as I age, but it has been an important option for me to embrace.

Of course, medications are not without unwanted side-effects. However, they are put through clinical trials and are likely safer than any street drugs you can get—which are often laced with God-knows-what. If you don't like the side-effects, it may be worth trying a different medication. That said, in the early stages of recovering from a psychosis it was necessary for me to endure the numbing side-effects of my high-dose antipsychotic so that my brain had the chance to heal from the psychosis. This is a really frustrating process and is not to be taken lightly. I had just endured insanity and then I was forced to deal with the flatness and depression that came from being on this medication. It was important for me to realize that I was going through immediate pain for an ultimate good.

Some of the medication I took caused weight gain or panic attacks, but all of this was a small price to pay for what medication has given me. Although the cons were significant, the pros ultimately outweighed them. I had a new life. I would tell you what I'm on if I thought it would help, but everyone is different, and will be affected differently by each medication. To find what works for you, you need the guidance of a good psychiatrist.

The for-profit aspect of pharmaceutical companies can be very problematic. I recognize that. It's not a perfect system but has been a good option for me. It's also important to note that tackling the root cause of our issues is important, and often there is some element of trauma that needs to be addressed. For me it's been a combination of pharmaceutical solutions as well as psychotherapy (CBT, cognitive behavioural therapy) that has helped me recover.

I can't stress this enough: everyone is on their own journey to find what works for them. We do this with ours and other people's boundaries in mind. Some people don't take pharmaceutical medication and are doing very well in their recovery. What I am saying here is not medical advice. This is my experience, though I believe I would be dead if it weren't for antipsychotics.

A New You

I know a lot of people worry that taking medication will fundamentally change their core personality or change their brain in a way that alters their essence. I get it, these things are scary. But in a way, that's kind of the purpose of meds, to change you, because the "you" that you are right now isn't working.

That's not to say you should feel ashamed for being that you, or that there aren't parts of you that are to be protected and celebrated. It's a matter of knowing what's in and out of your control and how that relates to the direction you want to go. What you should accept and work on, and what should be abandoned as superfluous to your core—these are for you to decide, for you to choose. Or, you may choose to sit with the vulnerability that there are parts of our essence that only (the) God(s) are/is aware of, a stance which helps some people be more considerate with their actions.

It's important to acknowledge that everything we do changes the brain in its own way. Are some changes irreversible? Yes. But it's incredible how malleable, how plastic the brain is. "Neuroplasticity," as it's called, is fascinating stuff.

This idea that we have an essential nature (a soul) is one you may or may not believe. It's not my place to tell you that you're wrong or preach that all personality resides and is dependent on the brain. At this point I'm sympathetic to various viewpoints. I know that when I was first hospitalized, I remember waking up in the unit and feeling fundamentally different than before. It became important that I was open to accepting this new me (which included mourning the old me).

Consider this story. For those who celebrate it, Christmas is an emotionally loaded day. I have strong memories of the Christmases of my youth, but those Christmases are gone now, my parents are divorced, my sister and I have grown up. A way to enjoy days like these more, and not get stuck holding on to something that we'll never have again, is by letting them be something new. Be open. I feel like a lot of life is like this; we must adapt to how we and the world change, and to the new chapters in our lives. If we're too busy holding on to an idea of who we were or who we think we are, we'll miss out on who we could be.

The Essential Self

As for myself, is there something that stays the same amidst all the changes in life? What's essential, for me to be me? I don't mean the things I have or hold like my mental health diagnosis, my memories, or my interests. I mean the person having and *holding* these sorts of things. Am I what's left when my thoughts are gone?

There are some great interpretations of what we are. Carl Sagan spoke of us being the universe looking at itself (34). That's really beautiful to me. You could also look at us as if we're light, if light is how we see things and not a thing itself.

I also find it interesting to consider how we can be seen to exist outside of our physical self, how our identity is defined and embodied by the groups we belong to. Who I am extends past my body, but within my body there is also the foreign element of my subconscious. It's me, but a mysterious part of me that offers suggestions that have motivations I'm not always aware of. Having aspects of my identity that I don't choose feels vulnerable. My control isn't total in that I not only create myself, I discover myself as well.

So if there is something else that plays a hand in defining me, and I also define myself, there is in a sense a dance in life between receiving cards and choosing how to play them. We make our clocks as a reaction to time. We make the markings *3 o'clock* to represent the essence or abstract object which is 3 o'clock. *Our* essence, *our* continuity, some would call it a soul—it's either a fiction created by us, or the centre of our being.

I am a creative spark that directs as well as is directed. Then there are clocks, which are objects, or maybe demonstrate a system, a set of abstract objects. But a story, which relates to that spark of my mind and/or soul, a story isn't a traditional object, and may not be any sort of object at all. A story can have an *infinity* of interpretations, and so defies any attempt of ours to objectify or essentialize it completely.

The Ship of Theseus

The Ship of Theseus is an ancient Greek thought experiment (35). With the Ship of Theseus, we ask, if you change a ship plank by plank—at what point is it a new ship? The root of its relevance has to do with multitudes of "being" as opposed to "being" that is unified. The unity/essence that is the ship was there, or is there a distinct "thing" called a ship?

What about the unit (unity) of our bits? It's a unit, but of what? A ship is not made of just planks; there are all sorts of other elements. What sort of steps are available when we shift from ship to ship? Is this a distinct amount, or is it infinite? If infinite, how can they be steps? If there are an infinite number of steps, we'll never get to being a new ship. Once you've divided something, how can you return to it? Is all this thinking far too linear?

To bring this down to earth, consider the pro-life/pro-choice issue. A pro-lifer's argument hinges on the existence of a soul, an essence, an important continuity that transcends the mundanity of dust (planks). Asking at what point this essence exists is akin to the same question of identity we have with Theseus's ship. At what point does this new identity/soul separate from the environment? Or do they not emerge from the physical? When does "it" become "them"?

Values

A value is an abstraction or a concept, an idea about something. It is the worth that we assign to something, the assessment of what and how much we think it is worth.

Social or ethical values can clash. Sometimes these clashes happen internally, like when you value good mental health but also value the pleasure you get from an activity that in the long run may be bad for your mental health. Some of the most painful value clashes happen externally, for example, within families. We all know the generational differences that make for frustrating and sometimes toxic interactions. A parent may value decisions that lead to independence and security, whereas a teenager may value decisions that enable new experiences and self-expression. Values change as we grow as people. As our environment and situation change, so does what we value.

Some values are held more strongly than others; their position in our overall set of values is higher than others. I value writing, especially when I'm feeling inspired to do so, but it can get in the way of getting a good night's sleep. Since I value getting a good night's sleep more, I make a compromise and stop writing at a reasonable hour and go to bed (most of the time).

Value clashes can be really difficult because sometimes our boundaries get crossed and we're left in compromising positions. We don't always have the control to avoid these situations, because sometimes it's our society's values that clash with ours. It's my belief, for example, that capitalism's value of profit over health can be really toxic, especially to those who are differently abled, those who don't fit into the traditional notion of usefulness. This is a difficult personal situation to be in. We can't control certain things in life, but at least we can control how aware we are of what we stand for, and do what we can to diminish whatever is compromising our values. How evangelical we are about this depends on the person.

It's an interesting exercise to map out your values: in a lot of ways they reflect or are a big part of you. When you lay things out, you can see if you're living according to your values or if there are changes you'd like to make. If you notice that there are values clashing, it's helpful to see that, to wrestle with it, and see if you can come to a resolution. It's also interesting to consider things you don't value, or things that you oppose. If you're taking part in activities that go against your values, you could set some goals to change that.

What about values you *want* to have, things you'd like to add to your set of priorities or to your belief system? Externalizing these things can be hard to put into words or it may even be stressful to see existing values you didn't realize you were disregarding. Although it can be a difficult process, I find things like journaling to be super helpful in organizing my thoughts. So often, things swirl around in our heads in an awful repetition, and we're not quite aware of the intensity or frequency of our thoughts until we write them down. Talking things through is another great way to make our thoughts accountable to reality. Going through these processes on our own can be overwhelming, so doing them with a mental health professional might be the right option for you.

I value being able to express myself creatively, being kind to others, connecting and spending time with family. I feel like these three values are equally important to me, but writing them down has made me consider my relationship to creativity and how my obsession with it affects my relationship to my other values. I've learned from this process.

Now that I'm aware of this, if I want to, I can make choices that better reflect how I want my values to sit. If we're not aware of an issue, we can't consciously change it. Being aware of certain things can be painful, and so we may have the tendency to push those thoughts away and make things worse. I suppose you could say that we have to value having values, though I would argue that having values is unavoidable: it's just a matter of whether we're conscious of them or not.

If we learn to critically integrate unconscious offerings or things "running in the background" into our consciousness we can become more balanced and aware.

Boundaries

- Respecting your boundaries means removing yourself from situations where your values are being compromised
- Respecting your boundaries means sharing personal information with the appropriate friends and not with strangers (depending on your art, this can be hard for artists)
- Respecting your boundaries means not taking responsibility for things that aren't your responsibility
- Respecting your boundaries means saying no when you want to say no
- Respecting your boundaries means realizing that you have your own values and other people have theirs

Sameness/Difference

In tending to our mental health, something that's good for one person may not be for another. Maybe one of the hardest obstacles we have in mental health is that everyone is so different and has such different frameworks and chemistries. But aren't we all made of the same stuff looking at the same things? I have a friend who went into the woods with someone else. It was late at night and they were both looking at the sky side by side. My friend said, "You know, looking at these stars and constellations, I can't believe how anyone doesn't believe in God." His friend replied, "You know, it's funny that you mention it, because I was just thinking, looking at these stars and constellations, I can't believe how anyone could believe in God."

A Good Life

You're probably familiar with what is known as "the golden rule," and that is to "do unto others as you would have done unto yourself." An issue some people have with this rule is that you shouldn't assume that what's good for you is also good for someone else. What's done may be an imposition to the framework or belief structure of the other person.

How similar are we *really* though? We seem to have the same physical needs, but do we have the same mental ones? A good life for an atheist doesn't include being in a relationship with a deity, whereas being in a *real* relationship with a God is a cornerstone of importance for other people.

We have different values because we have different experiences which inform the filtering and framing that our mental canvas does. We're not a blank slate, but a process that affects what we're interpreting. Each of our speculations as to what is a good life is rooted and born from the communities we belong to. We build or find maps that conceptualize what we should avoid and what we should move towards. How we draw the line as to what "us" is and what is "other" is controversial. Here we have the basic elements of story, what is morally negative and positive, who are the heroes and who are the villains.

There are certainly many different and conflicting ideas of what it means to live a good life. A monk removes themself from the world, while others' mission is to make it a better place by interacting with it in practical ways. How we approach life is affected by our vantage points, our social positions, our lenses. If you're born in the east, you'll likely be involved with or reject an eastern religion. If you're from the west, there's a good chance you've accepted or rejected some form of Christianity, or you'd likely be familiar with it. This is important to mention because these preconditions to our beliefs are often out of our control.

Although it's not the most obvious comparison, I like to think about how goodness relates to furniture. For example, there are many different kinds of chairs, but is there something necessary and sufficient for something to be a chair? What is a chair essentially? It's necessary for a chair to be something you sit in or on, but is that sufficient to define a chair, in that there are other things that people sit in that aren't chairs? What property do chairs have that are unique to chairs? They are their own "thing," aren't they?

Looking for what is universal to all chairs (or for what is a good life) may be an impossible quest. Maybe seeing each chair as a reaction to how it's being *used* is what's important. Every chair is different, just like all our ideas of what's good are different, because we're using these things and pseudo things for different purposes. A good chair is one that facilitates sitting well, for the person or people who will be using it.

Systems of good and bad are used differently by different generations. If you're from biblical times, your version of good is going to be different from the modern one because of your context, your perspective. "An eye for an eye" was once progressive, because punishments didn't use to match the crime. People would be killed for things worth less than their life. How much is a life worth ultimately? A dark game to play.

As for what's good and bad, we can determine what to move towards and what to avoid based on rules or consequences. Rules are determined based on consequences, and the consequences based on some sort of value system. Whose rules and consequences though? What view is elevated? Which "chair" is to be made or discovered as the essential one?

It depends on what our goals are. If we want power or to survive, that's going to inform what we think is good. If we think freedom should be valued above all else, our concepts of what is good will reflect that.

Another thing to consider about goodness is the fact that when someone is good to someone, in that instance the person receiving good is losing the chance to be the giver. If there is only one serving of potatoes left at dinner, someone has to be the one who takes it, while the other people get to be the good people who let that person have it. There is a deficit there, where the receiver is in a sense subjugated and the giver needs a receiver for the giver to be good. Here we have power dynamics.

On a different note, how could we cement our definition of what's good, without falling into a sort of "never-ending chain of definitions" dilemma, where good is good because of this, which is because of this, which is because of this, etc.

If truth is solely based on evidence, aren't we left with that infinite regress? Thankfully we can say that some things just *are*.

Much of math, when it's broken down, comes down to "common sense" axioms. This is because of that, that is because of this, this, well, this just is. Maybe goodness is the same, in that at some point it just is. There seems to be a narrative trajectory towards there being less physical suffering in the world. This is a good thing.

Good for the sake of goodness: isn't that better than trying to align it with something else? Isn't it less good to want to be good because of fear of punishment or because of a sense of duty? These things have outside validators. Do they dilute the good?

It's hard though to trust any ultimate declarations of what good is without considering how their view is shaped by their experience. It isn't possible to conceive of goodness let alone anything else without having those conceptions filtered through what we've already lived. What goodness *is* a priori (without our experience) would be a wonderful question to answer, but this is unfathomable without using tools that both facilitate and distort the process.

We seem to be inescapably creative with our viewing, and by that I mean we are involved in determining the content based on how we frame and figure it. I know that my name is John Gerrard based on that identity being my choice. What I really want though is to know who I am when I'm not looking, or rather when no one is looking.

If knowledge involves pictures and pictures involve tools, this "looking without looking" would be like painting a painting without using any paint, without a frame and certainly no canvas, as these would all *add* to what I was aiming to capture, discover, relate. The material, the medium itself says things; the message itself is not material but requires the material to be realized.

Regardless of whether there is a lens that captures what goodness is without leaving our fingerprint, goodness, like meaning, exists whether we construct it or not. We can have good intentions to be good, but never really know the full implications of our actions. We can do our best to learn them, and some of us are more invested in this than others.

What is the purpose of a person being good in the world? Is it a way to help us survive, is it "just" that lens that's essential? I don't know, but I don't think so. I think goodness means taking care of people who wouldn't survive on their own, even those "outside of our wolf pack." In that sense, goodness goes against "survival of the fittest."

From my perspective, goodness is going against things being valuable purely for their utility. Goodness is an activity that's done because it's right, not because we're told to do it. There's goodness in understanding what a naturalistic fallacy is. Goodness is about collective collaboration and aiming to understand the inherent worth of life.

Maybe our perspectives form a system like numbers on a clock?

Good Art

We can say good art is art that realizes the artist's intentions, that it portrays or creates a universal. Good art may help us to project scenarios to move towards or to avoid, it may promote beauty or take a stand against injustice. To speak most generally, good art involves successful bridging and integration; it's the platform we walk towards each other and ourselves with. It helps us process things personally, as well as communicate our personal worlds to others.

Valuable Art

What makes art valuable? What makes it worthwhile? Is it in the process of making it, the feeling or release you get when you move the brush, the pencil, or your arms when you dance? Maybe it's because it helps us change, makes the often intangible nature of the goings-on in our minds tangible? Or perhaps its value is tied to what's produced and where it goes and who appreciates it?

Maybe the value is in what it instigates or inspires in us, in what comes next from it. Art can spark change or motivate a movement towards something worthwhile. Maybe its value is in the very fact that it has no concrete value, but is a luxury. It often isn't useful per se, and that is very valuable in a world overly obsessed with usefulness and utility. Maybe most of all though, art's value is in how dynamic and varied it is. It is many different things to many different people. It doesn't have any one essence, but is that which discovers and creates many.

Art and Control

At first an artist has control over what they present and leave out. They make choices, placing starts and finishes, erasing or not erasing. They pursue a direction and make new ones, but at some point they say it is finished, or say that it is never finished but you can "see" it anyways. Or maybe there is a giving up of control in the art process in that the artist taps into something that fills up the spaces it is allowed to inhabit? Maybe there is a negotiation of control with art making?

When an artist releases their work into the world, they are vulnerable. They abandon their control and make available their channelling. As an analogy, I have my intentions with these words. I am saying what I wish to say—but the words will say other things, won't they?

The Artist and Choice

One of my favourite quotes is, "If you wish to make an apple pie from scratch, you must first invent the universe," by Carl Sagan (36). I've made the quote my own by replacing the apple pie with painting. You can't paint a painting from scratch without first creating the universe. To me, this quote speaks to how interconnected and indebted everything is. It evokes the relationship between original, old, and new identities—how we should be humble when we make things, because there is always the "out of our control" influence of the universe around us, as well as the underlying and seemingly automatic parts of our psyche that help determine the choices we make.

If we define creativity as "something from nothing," we may only ever have the facade of this idea. We don't facilitate any true beginnings, because what's new is always owing and in relation to some preceding factor. Because of this we are never fully free to "start from scratch." Our newness is an extension of existing circumstances and materials.

This idea relates to our freedom and control. In making art as in living life, we are both free and unfree. I'm free (in control) in that my mental state seems to play a part in a variety of choices, and unfree (out of control) in that my mental state is restricted by the nature of what's already there internally and externally to work with.

We always have existing variables and propensities to reckon with, to react to. Before we start every piece of art, there is, metaphorically speaking, always someone handing us art supplies. Creativity begins with some determined factors, which make sense when thought of as choices determined by the artist. But when this determination comes from beyond the consciousness of the artist, this may seem to contradict our core preconceptions of what creativity traditionally entails—sovereignty, autonomy, and activeness.

Art isn't always a production though: it's also capturing, selecting, or highlighting what's already there. It allows passivity in the face of some other energy or muse. This unveiling, this discovery with as few footprints as possible, is in a sense scientific in that the aim is to observe and relay rather than to insert our own voice.

Perhaps our creativity lies in how we figure and frame what we discover? There is an interplay between input and output, with the artist in the middle. We react to variables outside of our control and determine their new shape. I find a card game metaphor helpful to illustrate this: we're given cards that we choose how to play. The rules of a game simultaneously both provide restrictions as well as facilitate the continuity of play, and that combination allows near-infinite possibilities for how the game proceeds.

In this process, as artists and as people, we have or don't have choice. These actions of control may not be conscious, or they may be ironic in that we choose to give up our choice. Still, we have a relationship to choice. I'm fascinated by that "other" part of self which seems to have its own motivation.

There seem to be preferences without the conscious realizing it: some of these preferences "we" become aware of, and some are forever outside our grasp. What system of priorities is my unconscious using?

Whatever those motivations are, we have the ability to step back and analyze. We can rethink what's been presented to us by the underground portions of our mind, and through this refiguring and recolouring we "play our cards." Our control of our unconscious consists of influencing it by our reactions. There is an internal conversation. We're receptive with our unconscious and then we make choices based on what's presented.

That is one way to analyze our situation, though there are many different theories and approaches to defining the self. There are academic perspectives, religious and spiritual perspectives, and artistic perspectives, all with their own biases due to what they do and don't focus on. Not everyone agrees that even with free will we have choice, with the hard determinists claiming that it is all a sort of sterile chain of cause and effect and that our experience of freedom is an illusion.

A materialist would contest that there is no reality other than the material, and that all emergent effects and causes can be traced back to granular material circumstances. Then there are the behaviouralists, who are true to their name in that they think we're best understood by looking at our behaviour. What's important isn't theory or identifying the mechanics of self, but the product/output of these mechanics. There are also the systems that have been proposed that partition us into egos/superegos and the like, and suggest an inherent architecture to our personhood. I'm doing this to a certain extent when I divide the mind into the conscious and unconscious. There's also the persistent idea of an immaterial soul, which is a hard thing to talk about with any precision. And there's the artistic view which often keeps things poetic and open. Today's psychological practices seem to employ whatever method works. In a sense this is akin to how we have different ways of making that are useful depending on what the artist is intending to make.

From what I've gathered from my limited time as a person, there is a certain futility in any attempt at presenting an all-encompassing definition of selfhood. I can define myself as I want while empathizing as best I can with other perspectives. I can make claims such as that we're doomed or lucky to be ephemeral, or part of something beyond, some divine clan. Either way, I'm not naive enough to believe that the story I arrive at is the full story, that I have the God's eye view on my being. How I would be defined outside of my lens is an absurd thing to try to imagine, like Kant's thing-in-itself (37). Knowing what am I when I'm not looking requires me to look!

It's difficult to define the mind, because we need to use a mind to do so, and if we compensate for the bias of our observational instruments, we eliminate what we're trying to observe. Because we are in some sense a mystery, this comes with a lack of control, and with lack of control comes a lack of choice.

At the very least I have the experience of choice in how I react to internal and external factors. It's important that I'm open to the possibilities presented to me, but also important that I allow the possibility that a suggestion is wrong or needs to be left open for future insight. Just because I don't choose what is presented doesn't mean I can't choose how to value it. As to what compass or system we use to decide which thoughts are to be dismissed or followed, that depends on our motivations and values. Perhaps a balanced life is found in having conscious motivations that are in harmony with our unconscious ones.

When we overmediate our thoughts, it can be like water building up pressure against a dam. In mindfulness traditions, we're taught to observe our thoughts as if they were floating effortlessly along a river. We're encouraged to view these thoughts without judgment. I see an analogy here with the passive portion of an artistic practice. We need a certain openness to grow our work; there needs to be space for it. As in a conversation, we listen but also talk. As for the active, there are the judgments or choices we make from the information that's available to us. We listen, we react, and then engage in an art-making process that can be both receptive and productive. Channelling as we work, a dance between being in and out of control.

Letting the thoughts flow with the water is a submission or letting-go of sorts, and we can gain a lot by giving up pieces of our control like this. Sometimes with art making, that control is given up by accepting restrictions, and I find there is an ironic freedom that comes with submitting to rules for making images. We can be paralyzed by having too much choice. Having confines or structure by limiting elements allows an order for other elements to thrive in. We can choose different variables to use, such as giving ourselves a timeline, only using certain materials, etc.

As artists, we make figurations and frame specific views; we use language and other symbolic systems to distort and reveal elements, lending an intentionality to what is otherwise unconscious or unseen. We work with existing tools to imbue and signify. We do this by making choices, and exploring parameters. The unknown is mediated internally and then becomes integrated as we re-create our conceptual world into the sensory one by making our thoughts into tangibilities. Then they are transmuted once more into thought, often very different in the minds of each viewer. An artist is found in between the visible and the invisible, interior and exterior, transforming elements as they react to the inputs of the physical and metaphysical world.

We are both in and out of control of life, and this is indicative of how we operate with creativity. The factors that are outside of our control are outside of our physical self, but also in our heads, in that we collaborate with a certain "otherness" within.

We listen to the work as it develops, making choices as reactions to the cards that we're dealt. These cards whose identities shift as they're shuffled, whose unfiltered form could only be found at the beginning of a universe. Then we play, and wait for a response.

The Difference Between Art and Science

Art and science are what we create them to be. Unless there are archetypal essences, known by the words *Art* and *Science* that we discover. Something beyond the shells of the letters, or what they evoke. Something beyond the signs of them that is essential. What sort of inherent and not imposed continuity do processes have?

How can we define these two things in stable ways? Or would a definition left open to change suit one or both better? What tools do we use? Do we define art scientifically or define art artistically? Do we define science artistically or science scientifically? Or is this a yin and yang sort of thing, in that there's some of one in the other and vice versa? Are they even on the same continuum? Is it proper for this continuum to be dualistic or am I missing (a) key variable(s)?

The sameness is that they're both tools to interpret perception, from inner and outer sources. Do they both aim for truth, or is art unrestricted by any goal or mission?

One way to look at it is to claim that art is a creative tool, and science a tool for discovery. However, art makes or leads to discovery and science is also creative, although it does its best not to be.

You can't have creativity without some sort of uncovering, and you can't have science without some remnant of the human hand, of their abstraction and symbolizing with theory and models.

Science is honest with the fact that a "finished image" for reality is not its role to accomplish. Scientists hold the truth in such a beautiful way, in that it's subject to change. Nothing is ever proven right, just a lot of things are proven wrong. It becomes quite likely that things are a certain way, but there is never that Truth with a capital T, maybe because science knows there's always some element of perspective (bias) in its discoveries.

Art can take "something" that is not yet tangible/sensory, and bring it into the material world by giving it shape, dimensions, duration, etc. Art can look at the tangible/sensory and make abstractions and representations just like science does. But science is aiming for accuracy and has a goal which is the truth, whereas art isn't limited by that utility unless it wants to be.

Science finds symmetries, what stays the same when other things change. The conceptual artistry in science is in the creation of models, theories, relationships from sensed phenomena. They aim to explain, much like a realistic painter tries to perfectly re-create a photograph, so there is no bias from the artist's hand. Though there is always some level of abstraction when we draw, even if that's just conversion from colour to black and white.

When we symbolize and move towards the abstract, where are we going? Are we being creative or are we discovering symbols from a realm that is non-objective? A scientific theory or model certainly isn't a sensory thing: it's built with and from other relationships, from abstract objects, and some connecting force. Are these essentials discovered or created? But maybe more importantly, could or should it be either/or?

Creative Discovery

I discover possibilities from my unconscious and make them tangible by relaying them to the page. This mental to the physical is where I'm creative, where there is choice in how I represent or abstract towards the non-objective zone.

It is such a privilege exploring ideas, shapes, and possible ideas inherent in shapes, and finding the music in and about spheres. I feel as if this process is home. Seeking stable structure, a somehow architecture, maybe mapping tips of the waves (38).

Everything is subject to change—ready to leap or negate elsewhere if that's what the cards tell me. It's a push and pull, a strange collaboration. Each piece is in a conversation with the last, and "willing" to speak to the ones that might come next.

Symmetry

That which stays the same amid change.

We Make Clocks, Not Time

Maybe time is like a river and I'm standing by its side staring straight across its wide waters. All I can see is what's straight in front of me; the past is gone and out of sight downstream. The future is on its way to the right of me. The three designations of past, present, future that help me handle all this time that's flowing by—did we invent them or are they inherent in some way to time or time's maker?

How about the concept of 3 o'clock? There is no such thing as 3 o'clock per se, that is, in a traditional material sense. Three o'clock is an abstract object or a relationship that we've either created to describe the phenomenon of time, or discovered as something primordially "given" to us. Another example is that of right and wrong. Are these distinctions, these relationships, "handed down" to us, or did we create these essences in response to our surroundings? What would it mean to create an essence?

The clock works with time relationships and together they organize time. The clock is a reaction to a segmented time, and segmented time a reaction to time itself. Our beliefs are responses to initial thoughts generated from our unconscious, and from those beliefs we live out actions.

We don't make the phenomena of time—and we may or may not make the concept of it—but we do have control in how we react to these things and pseudo things.

We don't choose the nature we're born into, the shapes we have to work with when we make our models, make our art. We choose how we build from the archetypes imposed, be they created or discovered. It's a clock that must be made, but the details are up to us. When we refigure the past to find a more realistic perspective, in a sense we are looking to build or find more precise or useful numbers for our clock.

Now how does all this relate to mental health diagnosis? Is there a system of "idea objects" as useful as our numbers on the clock are for time? How does this relate to personality systems, like the Myers-Briggs and Enneagram? What can I control? To reiterate my core question, do we find our labels or construct them?

Particular/Whole

How many different colours are there? I can look at the millions of light frequencies and divide them into distinct colour categories. You can divide the rainbow up in different ways, using more or fewer of these distinctions. You can then assign conceptual identity to those distinctions.

When we divide colour, personality, pathology into sections, how true are we being to each character? Is there a "right" way to do this? How can I say what's right without the holy grail of views (though the system we have for time seems to work very well)?

Language

Language's brilliance is in how it facilitates dynamic identities. "This is this, and also this, that too, and so on." Like how a pie chart can be segmented into sections, between each comma is a unity that is a part of a whole (39).

Hello, I am INFP / 4w5 / Cancer / Green & Yellow / Schizoaffective Bipolar Type / Lawful Good (40).

Labels

Labels aren't all bad, and they're not all good either. If a label is accurate it's a good thing. Often when we talk about labels, we're talking about stereotypes or categorizations that wrongfully generalize or leave out important parts of what's being labelled.

There is also the issue of labels creating the basis or justification for unhealthy action or non-action. If I am a certain personality type, am I therefore destined to perform certain behaviours? I could use my personality type to justify my spaciness or hatred of mundane tasks. Though should I accept my fate, in that I will always hate mundane tasks? And if a right-handed person uses their left hand enough, will they become left-handed?

This relates to the question of what is determined for us, and what is chosen. As soon as I identify myself with something, perhaps I then become it—which would mean I wasn't it before I "saw" myself as it?! We need to explore what we can and can't control.

Another thing to consider is how our actions reflect the group we subscribe to, or how the group we subscribe to reflects our actions. For some frameworks, if someone is a man, they therefore don't wear dresses. Is a person a man because they don't wear dresses, or do they not wear dresses because they're a man? How we define things matters, and there is a big difference between someone who thinks we create or construct these labels, and those who think we discover them as if they've been handed down by God.

Obviously, these are controversial issues, where we are often divided into sides that seem incompatible. It would be fair to ask though why it can't be compatible that both are true in some way. For whatever reason, it seems there is pressure to otherize the other side's perspective, especially for sex/gender and religion/spirituality. What is natural? Is natural a "construct"? (Would that be ironic?) Who decides what is natural? Isn't what is natural apart from our reductions of it? I'm not sure making a lens *the* lens can be done without wrongfully degrading or subjugating another. Thank goodness we can find sameness and integrate our lenses with our art and our literature. I imagine a canvas (collage?) so wide and deep that our additions are never at the expense of another voice. To be heard and represented properly: there is great comfort to be found in this.

Having a label that fits can be validating and feel good. It's that feeling of pride we have for our countries, that sense of belonging. A last name is another example, our sense of pride for our family, our genetics: it's deep-rooted.

In mental health diagnoses, labels can far too often be used to dismiss. I am schizoaffective so shouldn't be taken seriously; she has a personality disorder so she's doomed. That man is crazy; he does not belong to our family. Labels can seem to impose a destiny.

For some people, a diagnosis can feel like a death sentence. Do we change the label, make it more nuanced or do we not need one? Labels can be useful, and can serve as a map for what we're going through. How accurate are they though? Mental health ones shift and change with each version of the diagnosis book. While labels can serve as maps for our lives, and for other people's lives so we can understand them better, they can also mislead. I like to have a certain openness to future possible descriptions. This openness honours the nuance and complexity of character. There is always a portion yet to be defined.

I need to figure out what labels fit for me, what doesn't fit, and what is in-between or hard to say either way. I need to allow myself room for other labels, and not to let one smother me.

Diagnosis

It would be helpful to have fully accurate diagrams that describe our mental illnesses. Organic distinctions. A sureness with this has proved to be elusive, as our mental health diagnoses shift and change as our understanding of what they point to evolves (41). Their accuracy and/or usefulness in care is debatable because so often people are misdiagnosed. On the flip side, it can be comforting to have something to point to that explains why we are the way we are, and they can serve as a sort of map for our care. A diagnosis is useful if it's accurate, but we don't want to use it as a justification for negative behaviour that is ultimately in our control. This knowing of what is in and out of our control is important, because it informs the story we tell ourselves about ourselves, and that story often dictates who we become. We don't need to accept the negative associations people make with our diagnosis. Stigmatization can be crippling, and move us to believe we're bad people because of the label we've been given.

It's also all too easy to be in denial that we have a problem when we can't see what's wrong with us in a physical way. When you have a tumour, you can see it in an X-ray. When you have psychosis, there isn't that sort of evidence. It could be just how you are and perfectly normal. You think I'm sick? By whose standard? Prove it! Defining what's pathological/ dysfunctional becomes an all-too-subjective exercise.

If we could say definitively that there is something in the body going against the natural order of it, people would likely take it more seriously immediately, not to mention the other advancements in care that this would imply. When there are no physical markers, and all we have are symptoms to observe, it makes that illness harder to treat. Of course, claiming to hold a normative "natural order" of the mind is problematic to say the least.

Despite/Because

I'm searching for stable definitions of variables so I can better understand myself. Which cause is leading to which effect? What are the contributing factors and obstacles? Am I creative despite or because of my illness? If because, is *illness* still the right word for it? I've learned that this black and white, either/or thinking isn't appropriate, much like having one label or lens for an experience is rarely enough to honour its complexity. We find better accuracy when our views share a sameness. When there is overlap, it makes for a more stable picture.

Something can be an obstacle in an immediate sense, but a positive factor in a more ultimate sense. For subjective matters, the identity of what's in question depends in part on the perspective it's viewed from. What it is without observation is an absurd notion, albeit an alluring "view" to chase.

From one view, my sickness gave me something to overcome, and that strengthened me. The gaps in understanding of myself fueled me to bridge them. My symptoms, my shaky hands—this all informs my art. What I am doing is not done *despite* these things: these things are a part of it. The crooked lines are not a flaw, they are a feature; they reflect the organic nature of my life.

On the other hand, I make work despite the hardships that could have stopped me. I did not need them, but I made the best of them. I found solace with them. The character that emerged because of it is inseparable from my creativity now. This either/or is unrealistic; it's an imposition because of its reductiveness. There are different lenses to see things with. From some of these perspectives I am creative despite my illness, though from other perspectives I am because of it.

What do we call that which underlies and is pre-sickness or pre-health? What is the sameness among creativity, spirituality, and psychosis? Some yet-to-be actualized, yet-to-be judged spirit. If I lost what facilitated the unbearable paranoia, would I also lose what has led to my talents? Maybe what leads to suffering can also lead to a beautiful sensitivity, creativity, and maybe the spirit which is disconnected can also be connected in a big, bold, beautiful, and harmonious bliss.

If we're to "cure" mental illness and defeat that awfulness which sits so far to one side of the spectrum of experience, we should be careful not to lose the brilliance, the magnificent wonder we gratefully hold so far to the other side.

Insight

Insight is one of the best tools we have to help communicate what's going wrong with us, and therefore help the doctors understand what needs to be fixed. If we can learn to identify properly, be more mindful of what's going on inside our heads, we'll be much better off. Insight is the antidote to delusions. We need to recognize that something is wrong in order to change it.

In my experience, this is easier said than done. Things like social anxiety and psychosis can seem to overlap. Was that mood too happy or normal? Being a doctor is a hard job, having to figure out the picture (constellation) based on the clues we give them. But we can make their job easier if we work to use accurate words for their corresponding phenomena.

As I've mentioned before, meta-thinking is a great tool for recognizing what is going on in our minds. Stepping back. Thinking about our thinking. Writing things down has been super helpful for me, and can be a good way to process what I'm going through too. Insight can help us see the decisions we're making that are taking us somewhere we don't really want to go. It can also help us be honest with the thoughts we have that tell us we're something that we're not.

But when we're sick it can be hard to do these things. In a way, and with some sicknesses, having the motivation to look within and record ourselves, is what we're trying to fix to be able to do. The catch-22 applies again. I've said I need to record my symptoms to eventually feel better, but I need to feel better to be able to record my symptoms.

There is hope though. The more we push ourselves, and the more behaviours we carry out, the more motivation will come our way. This is not to shame anyone who isn't able to do this, as it may feel like it's impossible. Be easy on yourself and try something else to spark some brain changes that will lead to more joy, more purpose, and most importantly, less overall suffering.

Projection

If I set my sights, I know where to go. I might get sidetracked, and it likely won't be a straight line to get there, but I know the direction that my insight found which matches my values. When I project, I say this is a possibility. When I choose the right projection to follow, I say this is what I want, not what I want to want, but what I really want. I can take steps to get there. It might not happen overnight, but there are ways for me to find this which I deem successful, bit by bit.

Success

You never really know how hard someone is trying, do you? How much their muscles have to work when they "swim upstream," or how willing they are to jump in the water. Will is a hard thing to observe and define, as we use it to observe and define. Are the people to be most celebrated the ones who travel the furthest distances for their success? Some people can imagine the goal at the end of a great distance better than others, which makes the distance less of a distance by giving the person the motivation to cross it. Being able to empathize with the future is a great gift.

I have a paradigm I'd like to share. I've simplified people into two sides, the "left hand" and the "right hand." The left hand believes people are successful or not because of the circumstances they're involved with—the privileges or lack thereof. Their social position. The right hand believes people are where they are based on their own merit, based on their choices and essential character.

There is no left hand and right hand though, per se. Metaphorically, there are human beings with hands. If we were only at the whim of what's thrown at us, you wouldn't see people overcome their circumstances. But maybe there is no overcoming, and any success was always meant to be so? As Einstein said, God "does not play dice" (42).

I find it really annoying when people tell you how they rose to fame or success as if your circumstances were the same as theirs and there wasn't a significant amount of luck involved with these sorts of things. Factors out of your control. Maybe success is found in knowing what is in your control and what isn't? Knowing *yourself.*

Defining success is hard. Like everything else, we should be kind about it. Aren't we past everything being for survival, or is that naive? Talking about what's successful and what's not can get dark really quickly. You run the risk of valuing some lives over others. Think of the folks who can only move their eyes. The card deck(s) of life is/are varied and deep with all sorts of glory and misfortune. We can say having an illness is a bad thing without devaluing the identity of the person who has it. I have a type of bipolar; I am not bipolar.

Language matters to me, because in a sense we become the essences of the words we use, the masks we wear. I am not my thoughts, but my thoughts influence me. We each have our own idea of what success looks like. For me, it would be to offer something useful to this world. Maybe though it's enough to just exist. That's a nice thought, to be enough as is without needing external or some sort of conceptual validation.

Self-Esteem/Self-Compassion

Maintaining a healthy self-esteem has been difficult for me. Psychosis has a tendency to drag me too far in either direction. When I'm in an episode I'm flying too high, and when I'm not I often feel the shame of having been delusional, or I'm depressed and self-deprecating. Maintaining a balance where I'm confident and grounded is healthiest, and I'm happy to say I'm much better at it.

Self-esteem is different from self-compassion in that the former is about valuing yourself in a positive way. There is such a thing as having too much self-esteem or thinking too highly of yourself and believing that you're better than everyone. But I don't think you can have too much self-compassion. I think this is because it can be self-affirming and selfless at the same time. If you're kind to yourself, you can be kind to others. You have to know kindness to spread it.

There are, of course, horrible things that are hard to forgive, but being kind and forgiving ourselves don't give us the right to repeat the same mistakes. Part of forgiving yourself should be learning from that mistake. Shame, on the other hand, is rarely a productive way of preventing future offences. We don't want to label someone a deviant and have them resign themselves to the fate we have given them. If someone believes they're going to hell, they may feel justified to act in the way of someone who's going there.

The stories we tell ourselves about ourselves really matter. They are how self-esteem is constructed, deconstructed, and reconstructed.

There are times when I feel ashamed that I haven't worked a traditional full-time job for a lot of my life. This affects my self-esteem in a negative way. It may be western society that I'm at odds with, because it values usefulness so much. Is my worth really dependent on my job or career? What if I had a physical and not a mental difference in ability? Would society view me in the same way? I work really hard at my writing and my art. Why doesn't that feel like enough sometimes? These are the questions I ask when I'm getting down on myself for not being more capitalistic.

Everyone is thrown into different circumstances, and you didn't choose to have your abilities mismatched with what mass culture values. Even if you did choose to be this way, that's your prerogative. Yes, there are consequences, but maybe there's something wrong with the culture you're a part of, and not with you? Does the individual define what the group should be, or does the group define who the individual should be?

Having said all this, society wouldn't function if everyone was the same as me, or if everyone was the same as anyone for that matter. I really believe that most people want to contribute though. I think we should have jobs that match our abilities. For the jobs that no one wants to do, maybe we should reevaluate whether we should have those jobs, or pay those people more? That would solve issues of incentive.

People are valuable and belong in humanity with or without so-called "usefulness." To say anything different is regressive and objectifies a person into a role, into a card and not a card player. However, to humour the "everyone has to pull their weight" argument, I would like to introduce a hypothetical "artist's position." Let's say that part of the artist's role is to produce "what we enjoy at the end of a long work day," to spark and inspire, and to keep people existentially well. Let's say we only want to pay for "good" art. But knowing whether something is good, immediately and ultimately, would be a strange thing to try to measure. And then do we support only the artists who make something society thinks is "good"? Who decides what's "good," the algorithms, the influencers? They may claim to, but none wield the ability to see things without the distortions that come from seeing them with human eyes.

Let's pretend we found some essential lens that determines what is good and bad art. Those artists would have needed support to have made so-called good art, so giving them the support only when they've made "good art" is a bit of an absurdity. Maybe, using this logic, since we don't know which artists' work is going to resonate and survive, we should support them all? It's analogous to everyone wearing a mask during a pandemic even though they'll only be directly preventive in a minority of instances. We don't know which people are a part of that minority so we all wear masks. We don't know what art is going to be good, so we support all artists.

This is all based on a faulty premise though, that art has to be "good" to be valuable. Apart from being useful or beautiful, the personal relief we get from art is valuable, how it connects communities, helps us integrate and process our internal and external environments. These things are good in their own right.

Artistry is very valuable to me. I've been obsessed with being creative for almost 20 years. It's more stable than other things, but maybe it might have become "self-care" to excess, as the ultimate implications of not being more financially focused are bound to catch up to me. Does this make me irresponsible?

Even if this part of me falls short of who I want to be, I try to remind myself that I'm allowed the complexity of character, that I'm not monolithic one way or the other, nor could I be. Part of being the dynamic being that I am means that I'm not simply a success or a failure. I'm a person, somewhere in between and with other defining features and factors.

Of course I strive to be better, to work with what I can control and be closer to the good end of the spectrum. I'm differently abled in some ways, but "traditionally abled" in others. With this ableness I believe that I have a responsibility to give back. Because I'm able, I do my best to produce value for people. Because I'm built differently than a lot of people, I have to keep that in mind but continue to do the best that I can. I don't want to use that as an excuse or as a label that holds me back from contributing, but I do want to be realistic and accept myself as I am. I was born with a propensity for mental illness. I didn't choose that, and didn't realize the implications of my decisions that activated it.

I try, but the ultimate implications of my choices are hard to predict, hard to realize when I'm making them. It's also hard to know if I could have "tried harder" or "made a better choice." I need to give myself the benefit of the doubt, because believing that my character is more "good" than "bad" is a way for more good to appear.

It Doesn't Happen Overnight

If you're really sick, getting well doesn't happen after one therapy session, one pill, one run. But this works the other way too. Typically people don't go to bed perfectly sane, and wake up pounding their chest and screaming through the streets. Taking certain drugs can bring on a sudden psychosis, but that's a separate issue beyond the scope of what I'm writing about.

Chipping away at the stigma of having experienced psychosis is so important. If people aren't ashamed, or worried about being outcasts, then there's a better chance of them seeking support before things become extreme. It's going to take some time to get there, but I hope my writing can help move us towards balancing the narrative on psychosis. Yes, absolutely, there are some gruesome and tragic cases out there. I have my own perspective on personal responsibility, and lean towards solutions involving prevention of future crimes and not punishment. However, if one of my family members was seriously harmed by someone who was psychotic, my opinion might change like my perspective did. That being said, there are a lot of people, the vast majority of us who've experienced psychosis, who are just trying to live a good life like everyone else.

Over the years, I've learned what my symptom activators or early warning signs are. If I'm not sleeping, or if my writing is slipping into a "frantic manifesto zone," I know I need to make a change before things get worse. For me this usually means stepping back from work a bit, or reducing the stressful elements as best I can. Having good financial support options for people when they need to take a break would really pay off in the long run, so folks don't have to push themselves and get sicker.

When I'm feeling sick, people can't always tell. I've become pretty good at hiding my illness, out of necessity. If there was less stigma, I'd be more willing to tell people the truth of where I am. When I do tell the right people where I'm at, I usually get the support I need. I find my family has been mostly understanding. If the people you tell are supportive, they'll want to know what they can do to help. I recognize that it's not always a good idea to tell people that you've experienced psychosis. If you talk about it with the wrong people you could be minimized with a label and treated differently, treated poorly. We all have different relationships (or lack thereof) with friends and family. Your boundaries are yours to define.

It can be hard to bring these things up in the best of circumstances, as I don't like to worry people. Also, there's a certain vulnerability that comes from not being able to handle stress like "normal people" can. My lower tolerance for stress (among other factors) is part of why I feel outside of what society values. I do my best to stay firm with my own values. I'm able in some ways, not able in others. Does anyone else feel perpetually in-between?

Asking for help requires the insight to recognize that things are wrong. This is a lost resource when I'm deeply delusional, so it's important we take steps before things progress. Psychosis that's fully developed can be unpredictable and therefore frightening. We stay away from those who are ill with it for that reason, and also maybe because we're weary about supporting someone who isn't on our team, who chose to be where they are and "deserves what they get." Well, you know what keeps people away from the deviance we fear? Community. Support. Having a social position that isn't toxic. Having purpose and a place to put energy. But there is something else, isn't there? I'm not sure what to call it, but to leave it out would be dishonest. Because I've been too optimistic, haven't I?

Psychosis is not psychopathy—a lack of empathy is not part of the diagnosis—but are some psychoses really evil? Is that despite or because of it, though? I would say that if someone is psychotic, their "badness," if they have it, may just be more extreme. Psychosis itself is morally neutral.

This is me speculating though. Moral issues are hard. Why does it seem like some people are doomed to fail morally before they even have a chance to start? It seems to me that a person's moral compass is often affected by factors that are outside of their control. Being born into an abusive situation, into poverty, not having a way or place to express their energy. These things can be overcome, absolutely, but the odds become stacked against a person when their current environment is also toxic. It's not one thing necessarily that does it, but an accumulation of negativity, to the point where people don't want to be in society. They hate society. And if society has discarded someone, how can we expect that someone to be invested in society?

The solution is in community, in stories being told, in the integrations of our perspectives, in care, in giving people reasons to be invested in the world. In getting people help before things get a lot worse. In building resiliency so that we can withstand storms of unfortunate circumstance, unfortunate nurture.

Resilience and Self-Care

Having resiliency is having the ability to handle adversity without "running out of gas." We have a full tank so that if we need to drive across town to pick a friend up, we won't run out of fuel and break down.

I've certainly been in that headspace where I'm vulnerable to any sort of trouble. I've made it normal to exist on little sleep and food, and carried out routines that have put me at risk for relapse based on a certain fragility I've embodied. I've justified it by telling myself, Oh, I'm just an artist—this is just how we live. By using this narrative to justify toxic behaviour I'm allowing myself to exist in a toxic headspace. When I'm like this I'm more prone to misinterpreting people's intentions. I get easily offended. I feel like a victim. We want to avoid these headspaces, for obvious reasons. In video game terms, we want to build up our "health points." Using a financial metaphor, we need to set aside a rainy day fund for when we need it.

How do we improve resiliency? We care for ourselves! We do things that build ourselves up. We take care of our physical and mental needs. One of the best ways to build resiliency, and one of the most important forms of self-care, is to be mindful of the story we're telling ourselves about ourselves. It's so important to try to talk to ourselves with kindness, to treat ourselves like we would a close friend. There are certain things I've said to myself that I probably wouldn't say to an enemy. If you're having a hard time being kind to yourself, it's worth trying to find the root of it, in an emotionally safe way. I'm not so sure why we're so harsh on ourselves—maybe because we think we should have made better decisions in situations, because we think we've seen what we could have.

I might be open to endorsing being overly critical and shameful if it were to lead to an eventual good. But so often all those attitudes do is discourage us more, and maybe even enable us to make bad decisions in the future. We can act in personal and interpersonally toxic ways, because that's just "who we are." If you think of it as a truth that you're lazy and incompetent, you're probably more likely to act like that in the future. If you think of yourself as someone who is doing the best they can, with the cards they're given, you're more likely to do the best you can with the cards you're given!

The most important form of self-care isn't a particular type of self-care, but rather embracing and enacting the attitude that facilitates activities of self-care. It's important to make space to care for ourselves, in part as a rebellion against the industries that bombard us with cheap, frivolous, and artificial "solutions."

It's also important with self-care not to get too fixated on one activity or thing as a solution. You have to be careful that self-care doesn't become vice. I determined this based on the relationship to the activity/thing. I'm guilty of this with art and creative projects. I get super fixated on making something every day, so much so that I can forget about other important self-care tasks, the more mundane ones, like eating well and cleaning my studio.

If we take time to do things to take care of ourselves, we become able to take care of other people. So, in an immediate sense, it may seem like self-care is selfish, but more ultimately it has the potential to be selfless because it gives us the capabilities and energy to go pick up that friend across town. That's also what the gas in the tank is for.

The Past

Try not to judge past decisions as if you had today's information available when you made them.

Rethink Your Thoughts

Rethinking your thoughts isn't about putting a positive spin on everything, it's about seeing things more realistically, trying to see things with a balanced light. I can't be sure of what people think in reaction to what I say. I can't read minds, but I can try to reframe things while being kind to my past self.

My thoughts lead to feelings or actions. My actions lead to thoughts and feelings. My feelings lead to actions or thoughts. It's a triangle. Change your thoughts and you'll change how you feel and act (a tenet of cognitive behavioural therapy).

I have so much I want to rethink. I want to be at peace with my past like everyone else. I'm living a privileged life in so many ways. Had many sacred moments over coffee and cigarettes in all-night diners, vulnerable conversations in cars or vans as we drove. Rather, the night told stories while we drove. I've been understood. I've made friends laugh, but also said and done hurtful things. I'd like to think that I've said and done wonderful things too. May I be held accountable for the bad stuff, to prevent future offence but not for shame. May I erase the unrealistically negative judgments, and do this without replacing them with false optimism. I'll find that middle ground. Looking back I'll ask, Who is this human? Past lives where I pontificated like a pastor, so sure and basking in euphoria. Who is this person with Christian references tattooed on their flesh?

Rethinking My Christianity

I was a baby when I was first baptized, so it was done without my consent. My early years were church-influenced, but my family moved away from it once my father stopped going on Sundays. As a teenager I became quite involved with Christianity in what at the time felt like a progressive way, and was baptized again, by choice, at around 15. At the time, this wasn't religion to me, this was spirituality, a relationship with God. In retrospect that claim may have been just a clever marketing ploy.

This is the cynical side of me talking, I don't mean to degrade Christianity or spirituality, because I know that my truth is not *the* truth. I go back and forth between being sympathetic with there being a loving spiritual dimension to life, and thinking God should sooner be called an alien, in that they are impersonal and not necessarily holding our best interests at heart. When I was a teenager, experiencing God was mystical and profound. I had what seemed to be (or were) spiritual awakenings at conferences where I was so sleep-deprived, I heard Jesus. (But was it just the sleep deprivation? Is that the only appropriate interpretation?) There were people who were always worried that they never had a profound experience like this. They would probably consider themselves lucky to also have avoided the psychosis that followed my experiences.

My ethical teaching up to that point was mostly from my family and *Star Trek: The Next Generation* (43). I also really enjoyed listening to sermons, and to this day listening to people speak is one of my favourite ways to learn.

Christianity now seems to be a sort of "choose your own adventure." There are so many different interpretations of the Bible that getting to the heart of the gospel, the essence of Christ, seems rather difficult. To say "it's just love" isn't necessary and sufficient to define it, in my opinion. I'm skeptical these days. It may be impossible to fully see beyond your social positioning, though art certainly helps us integrate our views with others.

I can't help but wonder how much the message has changed from the original teachings. Greek, the language the New Testament was written in, wasn't the language that Jesus spoke (Aramaic). I suppose that's where the Holy Spirit comes into play, where there has to be faith that the essence is being received and translated well. Language is only accurate for so long before the phrases and references become foreign and too easily misread. I heard in a lecture once that if you want a completely accurate language you need a dead one.

But there is something very haunting about Christianity to me. I was devout at a very formative time in my life, and I suspect I will pray to this idea of God on my deathbed regardless of whether I identify as an atheist or agnostic for the next 50 or so years. This speaks to the mystery I feel about myself and life in general. There is this vulnerability of not knowing ourselves fully, our implications, that I've tried to speak to in this writing. We have immediates, first-person perspectives, but those ultimate lenses, those God's eye views we strive for, are always out of reach. The psychotic wrongfully elevates his subjective view into sureness, into a supposedly Godly one.

Two questions often get confused about spiritual matters. There is the question of whether God exists, and then the question as to what the nature or identity structure of that God is. I, as many others do, sit with the vulnerability of not knowing either answer. How is this reflected in how I live? I have room for other people's perspectives because there is an openness in my own.

Before the Bible was translated into the common folks' language, only the priests and the gatekeepers could understand it. People would "belong" to the church, but not fully know what they were belonging to. In a way that's how faith works, isn't it? You take a leap of faith in that you're trusting that your choice is correct without knowing it. But that's not how it was back then. Your religious framework just was. There were no alternatives, no choice about it. There must have been a sort of comfort to being submitted in this way, but unfortunately there was a substantial abuse of this power.

Of course, Christianity has evolved, to the point where it may seem strange to use the same overarching name for all its iterations. What is the essence of Christianity? There is what people say it is, and what they show with what they practice. I'm not a scholar or a theologian, and it's worth noting that these two perspectives are very different.

To me, in definition, the theologian represents learning with a lived experience of God, whereas the scholar is attempting that unbiased third-person perspective. Can we ever remove our bias with these things though? If we write about it academically, how can we capture the framework as it is lived? Shouldn't we include the lived-experience aspect of Christianity, just as when speaking about the mentally ill (or any framework or orientation, for that matter)?

There were a lot of great things about my Christian years, but a lot of emotional manipulation too. The shame that sex is often imbued with is incredibly toxic, the gender structures often appalling, and the smug "I have the answer" mentality nauseating.

Still I was accepted and cherished as a member of a community. No longer the runt or scapegoat of the group, I began to thrive socially. Belonging is so wonderful if we don't do it at the expense of another. I was sober then, happy and hopeful though not yet burdened with the stresses of death and lost love.

Rethinking God

I don't think it makes much sense for there not to be some sort of creator, in that every effect or situation seems to need a cause. But I don't think it makes sense for there to be one either. The cause-and-effect logic in itself is insufficient, as it induces an endless chain of who is the God of God, the God of God of God, etc. (44). I recognize that a lot of life is out of my scope. I can't see beyond the perspectives I've built and been given, beyond my place on earth. This is humbling. Maybe the eastern perspectives are more on point, in that we should focus on practicalities, like how to live, rather than grand theories or frameworks?

A lot of the time we impose spatial or temporal character on things that are likely beyond the spatial or temporal. On a similar note, if we're trying to find the gender of God—that's absurd. God is outside of gender: they made gender. But notice how I'm using "outside," which is a spatial characteristic.

Before time? Before is a function, a feature of time, so it's absurd to ask about things before time. Ultimately, it is difficult saying ultimate things well. We're limited by our particular perspectives, our social positions. Our images of

God always end up having some sort of human quality to them. There's that famous question of whether we're made in God's image or whether we make God in our image. One of my favourite quotes is from Voltaire: "If God did not exist, it would be necessary to invent him" (45). What I always come back to is wondering about the nature of ideas and mind, which to me seem like evidence of something that transcends the material.

As for experiences of the transcendental, I think there is an important distinction to make. Mystical experiences connect us to a higher power or to a mystery in ourselves, whereas psychosis isolates us and has us creating a reality of our own, or distorting reality into a toxic remix. Spirituality is a discovery of reality whereas psychosis is wrongly inventive with a sureness attached.

When I'm delusional, some intuitions come to me with such intensity I find them hard to deny. With my creativity I integrate my intuitions. I'm critical with them as I choose what to dismiss and what to accept. Throughout my choices and explorations I may not have found stable answers, though I'm refining my understanding of the questions. Dualism states that there are two different types of stuff, which is problematic. How do these supposedly different types of being translate into and from each other? Are mind and body aspects of the same thing, something more fundamental? It seems paradoxical that cause and effect coexist. It's seems strange that the world could be both automatic and with agency, be responsible for doing things and having things done to it.

Do we need to know the answers to these big questions to live a "good" life? Arguably, no, as a big portion of the world doesn't seem to really care, or they put their faith into a myth that "just is" for them. They say that we just don't know, but God knows, so it's o.k. Or some say we just don't know, but that's o.k. because we're getting along just fine. Maybe we'd be getting along better if we weren't so fixated on the beyond. We don't want to focus so hard on these things that we devalue what's going on in the here and now.

There's also the trauma that comes from religious conflict. It's frustrating to consider religions that have God(s) deciding who wins and loses. I mean, if you deem any of your kids to be fundamentally flawed, what does that say about your parenting skills? Old me might have been afraid that this is blasphemous to say, but I know now that if God's worth their name they won't be offended by my questioning, and hopefully they like the wrestling.

As for the problem of evil, some solve it by claiming that God shares their will with us. So whatever evil emerges is due to our choices, not God's. But what of the *propensity* for this evil? Evil is necessary for an ultimate good? Unacceptable.

I'm skeptical of there being one single answer to these sorts of things, because by claiming or aligning myself to a particular deity or framework I'm setting up a paradigm that seems to imply that someone else is wrong. How can I say if you're wrong or right if I haven't been in your shoes? This is a powerful thing to do when you think about it, deeming someone else's framework invalid. For truth to be worth its salt, it has to do this. These postmodern notions that everyone is right in their own way are so strange, that there are no universals, there is no God's eye view. Although, so is the notion that there is one essential or universal interpretation of our experience. Claiming there is a monolithic "way life is" has an eerie colonial feel to it.

I love philosophy but still have a lot to read to understand the history of dialogue surrounding these issues. I think I approach these things as a phenomenologist would, in that I try to focus on my perception, not the theories that have been built around these perceptions. From my understanding, there are these big elegant frameworks for existence that are true to themselves, but never quite grounded in reality, and then there are the people who deconstruct their notions. A reconstruction that showed what was necessary and sufficient with it all would be lovely.

Maybe all this navel gazing and focusing on what I believe is counterproductive though. I know about kindness: maybe I should just get on with it.

When Strange Things Happen

I've had a lot of meaningful coincidences in my life (46). I suspect we all have. Moments in songs I'm listening to matching up with what's going on in the world. Being on the verge of changing the subject in a conversation, when the person changes it themself to that subject. There are these moments, where we think, What are the odds?! I heard once though that there are so many incidents that it truly would be a miracle if some didn't collide, but I'm not so sure about that, as some things in life seem to be pointing to a bigger picture. It's one thing to say there are signs, and another thing to claim to know what they're saying.

When I was watching a basketball game with friends one time, the game went to intermission. This wasn't on TV; it was being streamed, and so the intermission was just a screen that said "We'll be back soon." We had been sitting there for a while, with this on the screen, when I suddenly had an intuition the game was going to start so I snapped my fingers. Lo and behold, the game started. I hadn't watched many games like this before, but maybe the unconscious part of me was counting in the background? I don't know. More importantly though, what could this possibly mean?

As my dad would say, "Well, that's all fine and dandy, but what does it have to do with the price of beer?"

I think that a lot of the time we forget what we say, or have heard, and so we can have moments where it seems like information comes from nowhere, when in reality it's just coming from another part of our mind. This part of us. That mysterious automatic. When I was in the depths of psychosis, these sorts of moments seemed so real. I was so convinced I was receiving messages, or that there were connections and bolstered significances that weren't there. It's as if you've seen evidence (you haven't), and that part of your brain that is skeptical has been falsely satisfied. It can be euphoric, and life can feel larger than itself. That being said, when it's paranoid thoughts, you certainly don't want that addition. And even when it's positive, it can be isolating and/or embarrassing when you level out.

With things like coincidences and connections, some are spookier than others. When you're delusional, things seem more meaningful than they actually are. By definition. But it's up to you to decide what means what, what's grounded and possibly shared, and what's just noise. The best way to do this, I find, is to have diverse sources of critical judgment and perspective, as well as keeping a certain openness about the issue. You don't have to completely disregard your views to do this, but if you're open, you leave yourself room to refine. As someone who has dealt with psychosis, I'm probably more skeptical than most because I know how off my perception can be. Because of this it's been hard to maintain a balanced approach to the things we can't directly observe, and it's hard not to want to disregard them completely sometimes. I always come back to trying to figure it out though.

Those moments where there are these samenesses, these symmetries. It makes me wonder if there is some semblance of order here after all.

Together/Alone

My creativity is a process of insight. A reaching for the awareness and acceptance of my place in this life. It's integrating my intuitions, a dance with that ocean overhead. With it I experience the ineffable, and try to foster an understanding of what has been given or imposed, and what I can change. I work to channel the fact that some moments have no correlating words, that there is no sign for the maker of the propensity for signs. I hope to have the freedom that comes from submitting to that, that if they exist, only they will know my name. Will it happen to be the same one that I've made? I hope to find those who connect that deep balance between our control and our belonging. With them light fills us and empties out the dread-filled dark.

Delusions elevate or degrade me away from these connections. They throw me deep into the sky as a lonely "ruler" of my own. They have me fall far down past the ground, as I'm suffocated by the enemies of my making. It's that sign! No, it's that sign! No, I feel it's that shell now! All done endlessly as if I'm in a realm of hungry ghosts (47).

Keep me away from that lonely scattered sureness. Today, tomorrow, and how I refigure the past. Help me move towards sharedness, towards some semblance of truth, towards knowing what I can and can't control. I may make signs, symbols, text, and images. Though these are merely like clocks for the time that's been given or imposed.

Psychosis Exploits Openness

Psychosis is an extreme sureness where sureness is unwarranted. I get suggestions that I cling to. Creativity itself deals with sparks, with suggestions, with integrating the unconscious self. This requires a certain openness, an openness that perhaps the psychotic part of me exploits. Creativity requires selecting from intuition and being convinced as to which to follow, but we know we're speculating, we should know it's not gospel.

These dark moments I've experienced, where my skill at speculating was hijacked. These experiences are a part of my story whether I like it or not. I think back on them a lot. Past moments pop into my head, seemingly out of nowhere. How bizarre that this person was me, how thankful I am to be away from him. I do my best to accept these thoughts and colour them in a more realistic light instead of repressing them, but I would prefer him to be superfluous and not essential to my identity. Learning how to rethink thoughts and with the support from my community, I'm where I am today, which is in recovery. This includes good days and bad days, but the bad days don't overwhelm me because I am resilient, and I know that no matter how bad, a day will always be temporary. It's amazing what letting go into a good night's sleep will do. Nature's reset.

Notes

(1) **"A part of me apart from me"** Bon Iver, "Holocene," side 1, track 3, on LP *Bon Iver, Bon Iver* (Bloomington, IN: Jagjaguwar, 2011).

(2) **I trust that my senses and intuition** Carl Jung proposed that we gather information with our intuition and senses (the "irrational processes") and make decisions with our feeling and thinking (the "rational processes").

(3) **Or does everything have some element of spirit or mind?** "Panpsychism is the view that mentality is fundamental and ubiquitous in the natural world." See: "Panpsychism," July 18th, 2017, *Stanford Encyclopedia of Philosophy*, https://plato.stanford.edu/entries/panpsychism/ ... If we substitute mind for spirit this could be seen to relate to animism.

(4) **It's o.k.** This is a reference to the triangle in cognitive behavioural therapy. When I'm feeling whimsical I imagine it's a sort of holy grail of its own.

(5) **I smoked cannabis in my early teens** See L. Arseneault et al., "Cannabis Use in Adolescence and Risk for Adult Psychosis: Longitudinal Prospective Study," *BMJ* 325 (7374) (2002): 1212-13.

(6) **Traditionally, when people use the psychopath label** *Psychopathy* is defined as a "mental disorder especially when marked by egocentric and antisocial activity, a lack of remorse for one's actions, an absence of empathy for others,

and often criminal tendencies." *Psychosis* is "a serious mental illness … characterized by defective or lost contact with reality often with hallucinations or delusions." *Merriam-Webster's Collegiate Dictionary*, https://unabridged.merriam-webster.com/.

(7) **You feel very sure** My hypothesis for delusions and related matters has foremost been influenced by my experience, though I've been exposed to other people's views by talking to doctors and reading articles and books, listening to music and watching film. Conversations with my partner Jennifer Greco (and our family) have shaped me and my philosophies greatly and this book wouldn't have been possible without their insight and intellectual engagement. Special mention to my genius sister Jennifer Findlay and parents (step and biological) as well as the philosopher Lauren Leydon-Hardy. My friend Dr. David Moore has been most gracious in answering my questions on Quora as well as sparking curiosity and luminosity with his own writing. Articles relating to psychosis and spirituality from *Project Muse* published by Johns Hopkins University Press were great reads. I'd like to acknowledge the sermons of John Nicholson as well as Jeremy Duncan and his non-violent interpretation of Revelation which was influenced by the writing of René Girard. The following books helped shape my views, if only indirectly: *On Stories* by Richard Kearney, *Jung on Art: The Autonomy of the Creative Drive* by Tjeu van den Berk, *12 Rules of Life* by Jordan B. Peterson, *Free Will* by Sam Harris *A Guide to the Good Life: The Ancient Art of Stoic Joy* by William B. Irvine, *Models of Madness: Psychological, Social and Biological Approaches to Psychosis* edited by John Read and Jacqui Dillon, *God: A Human History* by Reza Aslan, *Consciousness: Confessions of a*

Romantic Reductionist by Christof Koch, *Gödel, Escher, Bach: An Eternal Golden Braid* by Douglas R. Hofstadter, *The Pursuit of Meaning: Viktor Frankl, Logotherapy, and Life* by Joseph B. Fabry, *Big Magic: Creative Living Beyond Fear* by Elizabeth Gilbert, and *Panpsychism in the West* by David Skrbina. The *A Very Short Introduction* series published by Oxford has been especially informative, as well as the Great Courses series on Western Philosophy, Eastern Philosophy, Free Will, etc. the *Stanford Encyclopedia of Philosophy* has also been especially useful as has *Wikipedia.* I have undoubtedly missed sources here, so please forgive me if that relates to you.

(8) **In science, certain theories can be very likely** Inductive logic offers answers that are open to new information. "An inductive logic is a logic of evidential support. In a deductive logic, the premises of a valid deductive argument *logically entail* the conclusion, where *logical entailment* means that every logically possible state of affairs that makes the premises true *must* make the conclusion true as well. Thus, the premises of a valid deductive argument provide *total support* for the conclusion. An inductive logic extends this idea to weaker arguments. In a good inductive argument, the truth of the premises provides some *degree-of-support* for the truth of the conclusion, where this *degree-of-support* might be measured via some numerical scale." "Inductive logic," *Stanford Encyclopedia of Philosophy,* March 19, 2018, https://plato.stanford.edu/entries/logic-inductive/.

(9) **We can say that we think to survive** Philosopher Friedrich Nietzsche wrote about our "will to power," how our basic motivations relate to power.

(10) **Are there archetypes** This is one of my core questions. Is the nature of abstract objects or essences discovered or created? Pythagoras talked about everything being number, Plato talked of "ideal forms" existing outside of our universe and how we interact with "shadows" of them. Carl Jung talked about the collective unconscious and archetypes. Personality systems could be seen as a sort of "card deck" that offers us potentials that we elaborate from.

(11) **It's a beautiful thing in life** This conclusion is based on an interaction I had with Professor of Rhetoric (Emeritus) Frederick Dolan on the website *Quora.com.*

(12) **But it isn't** "Ideas of reference must be distinguished from delusions of reference, which may be similar in content but are held with greater conviction. With the former, but not the latter, the person holding them may have 'the feeling that strangers are talking about him/her, but if challenged, acknowledges that the people may be talking about something else.'" See: "Ideas and delusions of reference," *Wikipedia,* October 25, 2021, https://en.wikipedia.org/wiki/Ideas_and_delusions_of_reference.

(13) **Apart from medication, there are other ways to combat these misrepresentations** The *Wikipedia* article for cognitive behavioural therapy outlines its origins and influences ("Cognitive Behavioral Therapy," *Wikipedia,* November 15, 2021, https://en.wikipedia.org/wiki/Cognitive_behavioral_therapy). I learned a lot about CBT through an online group led by the psychosis centre at the Foothills Medical Centre in Calgary. The "percentage system" is from that course. They used material that is copyrighted by Nicola Wright and Sarah

Bertrim. There is also a known sameness between CBT and the ancient Greek philosophy of stoicism. "We are more often frightened than hurt; and we suffer more in imagination than in reality" (Seneca).

(14) **What other possible explanations** Nicola P. Wright et al., *Treating Psychosis: A Clinician's Guide to Integrating Acceptance and Commitment Therapy, Compassion-Focused Therapy, and Mindfulness Approaches within the Cognitive Behavioral Therapy Tradition.* (Oakland, CA: New Harbinger Publications, 2014).

(15) **When I think I'm crazy** See Anthony P. Morrison, Julia Renton, Paul French, and Richard P. Bentall, *Think You're Crazy? Think Again: A Resource Book for Cognitive Therapy for Psychosis* (East Sussex: Routledge, 2008).

(16) **One popular hypothesis** There are a variety of studies that tackle this question. Here is one of them: Solomon H. Snyder, "The dopamine hypothesis of schizophrenia: Focus on the dopamine receptor," *American Journal of Psychiatry* 133(2), 1976, pp. 197–202.

(17) **To quote Groucho Marx** A well-known quote from Groucho Marx, sometimes given as: "Blessed are the cracked, for they shall let in the light."

(18) **The flesh** Merriam-Webster dictionary calls asceticism "practicing strict self-denial as a measure of personal and especially spiritual discipline."

(19) **Thesis, antithesis, synthesis** This is the structure of a dialectic. A variety of people have expanded on these concepts, including Socrates, Karl Marx, and the German philosopher Georg Wilhelm Friedrich Hegel.

(20) **Imaginary/symbolic/real** Words made famous by the psychoanalyst Jacques Marie Émile Lacan. Some have compared these concepts to ones made by Carl Jung.

(21) **If you're interested** An abstract writing project of mine which explores opposites and potential resolutions between opposites. http://figuringframes.com.

(22) **I believe that this mystery** This belief could be seen to be related to the Jungian concept of individuation.

(23) **The first psychosis I had** I'm referring to the record *Mapmaker* I released under the moniker Francis Cheer (Well Sure Records, 2014).

(24) **I've heard that the best way to help someone** A great resource for those interested in how to help a friend or loved one suffering from psychosis: https://www.earlypsychosis.ca/how-to-help-a-friend-or-loved-one.

(25) **A high percentage of suicide attempts are unsuccessful.** For more information: https://www.cdc.gov/suicide/facts/index.html.

(26) **"He who has a why to live for can bear almost any how"** Friedrich Nietzsche, *Twilight of the Idols* (1888).

(27) **There are a few causes** This Australian health website was my source: https://www.healthdirect.gov.au/causes-of-psychosis.

(28) **Some have said we're incurable** I read the book *Models of Madness,* 2nd ed., edited by John Read and Jacqui Dillon (East Sussex: Routledge, 2013), which includes examples of some of the awful things that have happened to the mentally ill.

(29) **Reminds me of the book** Kyle MacDonald, *One Red Paperclip: How to Trade a Red Paperclip for a House* (Houston, TX: River Grove Books, 2007).

(30) **I should strive to be like the Buddha** The Buddha grew up in affluence but left his father's kingdom to discover the world. He became an ascetic, renouncing the pleasures of the world, but would eventually leave that tradition and support moderation with worldly pleasure.

(31) **Eye Movement Desensitization and Reprocessing (EMDR) therapy** David P. G. van der Berg and Mark van der Gaag, "Treating Trauma in Psychosis with EMDR: A Pilot Study," *Journal of Behavior Therapy and Experimental Psychiatry,* 43(1) (March 2012): 664-71.

(32) **One that works** A good resource: https://icy-health.com/5-senses-grounding-effective-for-anxiety/.

(33) **When things are really bad** See: "Diving Reflex," *Wikipedia,* October 8, 2021, https://en.wikipedia.org/wiki/Diving_reflex.

(34) **Carl Sagan spoke** "The cosmos is within us. We are made of star-stuff. We are a way for the universe to know itself." — Carl Sagan, from *Cosmos* (Random House, 1980).

(35) **Ship of Theseus** "The concept is one of the oldest in Western philosophy, having been discussed by Heraclitus and Plato by c. 500–400 BC … The particular 'Ship of Theseus' version of the thought puzzle was first introduced in Greek legend as reported by the historian, biographer, and essayist Plutarch." There are other versions of the concept, such as an ancient Buddhist one. See "Ship of Theseus," *Wikipedia,* November 16, 2021, https://en.wikipedia.org/wiki/Ship_of_Theseus.

(36) **If you wish to make an apple pie** Carl Sagan, from *Cosmos* (Random House, 1980).

(37) **How I would be defined** "In the *Critique of Pure Reason* Kant argues that space and time are merely formal features of how we perceive objects, not things in themselves that exist independently of us, or properties or relations among them. Objects in space and time are said to be 'appearances,' and he argues that we know nothing of substance about the things in themselves of which they are appearances." See: "Kant's Transcendental Idealism," March 4, 2016, *Stanford Encyclopedia of Philosophy,* https://plato.stanford.edu/entries/kant-transcendental-idealism/.

(38) **Seeking stable structure** I read this metaphor by Yohan John on the website *3 Quarks Daily,* https://3quarksdaily.com.

(39) **Language's brilliance** I first learned of recursion's relationship to language from Stephen Pinker's *Words and Rules: The Ingredients of Language* (New York: Basic Books, 1999). I learned more about recursion from Douglas Hofstadter's *Gödel, Escher, Bach* (New York: Basic Books, 1979).

(40) **Hello, I am INFP** INFP is my Myers-Brigg designation. Cancer is one of my astrological signs. Green and Yellow are my colours for the Insights system (which along with the Myers-Briggs system was derived from Jungian material).
Schizoaffective Bipolar Type is a diagnosis I was given a few years ago. Lawful Good is my Dungeons & Dragons alignment.

(41) **A sureness with this** I am referring to the DSM-5, the *Diagnostic and Statistical Manual of Mental Disorders,* 5th ed. (Washington: American Psychiatric Association, 2013).

(42) **Albert Einstein** The full quotation, which Einstein wrote in a letter to German physicist and mathematician Max Born in 1926, is: "Quantum theory yields much, but it hardly brings us close to the Old One's secrets. I, in any case, am convinced He does not play dice with the universe."

(43) **My ethical teaching** A couple of my favourite episodes are "The Inner Light" and "Darmok."

(44) **The cause-and-effect** This shows infinite regress, a problem also expressed by the "turtles all the way down" story from Hindu mythology. See "Turtles All the Way Down," *Wikipedia,* November 16, 2021, https://en.wikipedia.org/wiki/Turtles_all_the_way_down.

(45) **One of my favourite** This famous saying by Voltaire is "contained in a verse epistle from 1768, addressed to the anonymous author of a controversial work on *The Three Impostors,*" which is "a long-rumored book denying all three Abrahamic religions: Christianity, Judaism, and Islam, with the 'impostors' of the title being Jesus, Moses, and Muhammad (peace be upon him)." See "Voltaire," November 16, 2021, and "*Treatise of the Three Impostors,*" July 16, 2021, *Wikipedia,* https://en.wikipedia.org/wiki/Voltaire and https://en.wikipedia.org/wiki/Treatise_of_the_Three_Impostors.

(46) **I've had a lot of meaningful coincidences in my life** *Meaningful coincidences* is a term coined by Jung.

(47) **All done endlessly** One of the hellish realms in Buddhist belief.

Photo at Workshop Studios by Emma Palm

About the Author

John F. Gerrard is a multidisciplinary artist, with a focus on visual art. In his teens and 20's he was active creatively as a musician, touring across North America and playing locally. During this time he got his feet wet with visual art, doing graphic design work for bands and small businesses. John attended the Alberta College of Art + Design (now Alberta University of the Arts) with the intention of pursuing a design degree, but became obsessed with creating with charcoal and paint. He majored in drawing at ACAD and then went to work at a commercial sign company. In 2016 he left to pursue art full-time.

In 2018 John was trained by the Canadian Mental Health Association as a peer support worker. Since then he's been developing his art practice with mental health advocacy work. A highlight for John has been working with Branch Out Neurological Foundation, making images based on interactions with neuroscientists, and taking part in their charity events for three years and counting.

In 2019 he had his first international show in Chicago, USA as a part of the Some People Everybody exhibition. This multidisciplinary project examines the ethics, people, processes, and systems that constitute the maintenance of, and barriers to, health for human beings.